THE DATING, REDATING, AND REDATING AGAIN OF P52

THE P52 PROJECT

IS P52 REALLY THE EARLIEST GREEK NEW TESTAMENT MANUSCRIPT?

EDWARD D. ANDREWS

THE P52 PROJECT

Is P52 Really the Earliest Greek New Testament Manuscript?

Edward D. Andrews

Christian Publishing House
Cambridge, Ohio

Copyright © 2020 Christian Publishing House

All rights reserved. Except for brief quotations in articles, other publications, book reviews, and blogs, no part of this book may be reproduced in any manner without prior written permission from the publishers. For information, write,

Unless otherwise stated, Scripture quotations are from Updated American Standard Version (UASV) Copyright © 2020 by Christian Publishing House

A large section of the chapter on Philip Comfort and a few other places within THE P52 PROJECT is taken by permission from THE TEXT OF THE EARLIEST NEW TESTAMENT MANUSCRIPTS © Copyright 2019 by Philip Wesley Comfort and David P. Barrett. Published by Kregel Publications, Grand Rapids, MI. Used by permission of the publisher. All rights reserved.

THE P52 PROJECT: Is P52 Really the Earliest Greek New Testament Manuscript? by Edward D. Andrews

ISBN-13: 978-1-949586-10-7

ISBN-10: 1-949586-10-3

οι ιουδαι[οι] ...
ουδενα ι ν αο[?]
πεν σημα[ιν]ω[ν]
ση ηςκ[.]ην[.]
ριο[.] ο τ[..]
κα ειπ[εν]

Table of Contents

Preface 8

INTRODUCTION What is Papyrus 52 (P52) Rylands Greek P 457 11

CHAPTER 1 P. Egerton 2 15

CHAPTER 2 Paleography: The Criteria Used for Dating Ancient Manuscripts 27

CHAPTER 3 Colin H. Roberts and P52 43

CHAPTER 4 Philip Comfort and P52 59

CHAPTER 5 Brent Nongbri and P52 71

CHAPTER 6 Stanley Porter and P52 79

CHAPTER 7 Don Barker and P52 86

CHAPTER 8 Pasquale Orsini and Willy Clarysse and P52 93

CHAPTER 9 Elijah Hixon and P52 102

CHAPTER 10 Using Comparative Paleography to Date P52 .. 124

PHOTOGRAPHS OF THE EARLY MANUSCRIPTS 143

Highly Recommended Publication 167

Other Related Books By Edward D. Andrews 168

Bibliography 169

Edward D. Andrews

Preface

NOTE: Before beginning our preface, let me apologize to those who have extensive knowledge of this subject. I have repeated a few points throughout the book, a couple of points even four times. Why? It is repetition for emphasis. This book is not written from one Bible scholar to another. It is written for the churchgoer, the Bible student, the seminary professor, who do not have a deep knowledge of this subject. Lastly, there needed to be a few points that stood out, which are apologetic in nature.

What do the churchgoers, Bible college students, and seminary students do when one Bible scholar says one thing and another Bible scholar says something entirely different? As is the case with P52, several Bible scholars are saying different dates when the Greek New Testament fragment P52 was written? P = Papyrus (a plant in Egypt), the material used to make sheets of papyrus paper written on by scribes to make copies of Bible books. 52 = the number assigned to that discovered manuscript. What makes it even more alarming is when one is not an expert in the field of study, only having basic knowledge. How can they possibly know who is correct? Worse still, the Christian is embarrassed on social media to tell an atheist that P52 is dated to 100-150 C.E. Then the atheist responds to the Christian with, 'no, your evidence from 1935 is outdated, as recent research points to a date of 200 C.E. or later.' What is the Christian to do? What will be accomplished here in THE P52 PROJECT can be used at other times when the Christian is faced with two scholars or more offering conflicting conclusions. We are going to use the common sense that God gave us and weigh the evidence from both sides. We are going to treat THE P52 PROJECT like a criminal trial, with P52 being on trial.

P52 has been on trial for some time now. The new papyrologists, paleographers, and textual scholars have served as the prosecutor. They seek to convict P52 of being dated later than the initial dating of 100-150 C.E. Don Barker dates P52 to about 81–292 C.E., with Brent Nongbri dating it to 175-225 C.E., while Michael Gronewald dates it to 200-300 C.E. The papyrologists, paleographers, and textual scholars of old and some current have served as the defense attorneys. In many cases, the new scholarship has set standards of proof for dating P52 and other early papyri that far exceed what is reasonable and rational. Since we are going to play out this quest for dating P52 as a though it was a court trial, it should be noted that there are three primary standards of proof: (1) proof beyond a reasonable doubt, (2) a preponderance of the evidence and (3) clear and convincing evidence. Since we are playing this out like a mock trial, we would like to open with a statement before delving into the dating of and redating and redating yet again of P52. An opening statement is generally the first occasion that the trier of fact has to hear from a lawyer in a trial. The opening statement is generally constructed to serve as a "road map" for the factfinder. Here it is a measure taken to help the jury of readers to find the ability to look at the evidence objectively. Below we will use legal terms to define better how we should objectively view Bible evidence.

Legal Terms as to How We Should Objectively View Textual Evidence

The burden of Proof: The burden of proof falls on the one making the claims. If the textual scholar is claiming that P52 needs to be dated later, he has the responsibility to prove what he says is true if he is asked for proof. This proof needs to outweigh the evidence presented for the initial dating and other evidence for the early dating established since. I believe that the legal burden of proof offers the best answers to the issue at hand. Even with circumstantial evidence alone, a criminal can be convicted of capital murder and receive the death penalty. Below we list the levels of legal proof and some percentage and wording to indicate the degree of certainty it carries.

Warrants Further Investigation

Reasonable (30%): This is a low-level burden of proof in that it is enough to accept something as reasonably likely, being so unless proven otherwise by a more in-depth look, which may bring in more evidence. For example, at this level, it is reasonably likely that P52 dates to 100-150 C.E.

Probable (40%): This is also a low-level burden of proof in that it is enough to accept something as likely being so unless proven otherwise by a more in-depth look, which may bring in more evidence. At this level, it is expected that P52 dates to 100-150 C.E.

Conviction for Claim

The preponderance of Evidence (51%): This is a higher-level burden of proof that makes it more likely to be true than not true that P52 dates to 100-150 C.E.

Clear and Convincing Evidence (85%): This is an even higher level of burden of proof that P52 dates to 100-150 C.E., substantially far more likely than not.

Beyond Reasonable Doubt (99%): This is the highest level of burden of proof that P52 dates to 100-150 C.E., being beyond a reasonable doubt. It must be understood that feeling as though we have no reason to doubt is not the same as 100 percent absolute evidence of certainty. If one has doubts that affect their certainty of belief, it is not beyond a reasonable doubt. This, too, must be qualified. It is reasonable to have doubts about certain aspects of the whole, as they may not have all the answers as of yet. However, it does not affect the level of certainty as a whole.

We should also take note that Unrealistic expectations are unhelpful expectations. We have now heaped doubt on the Christian community when we set aside reasonable, rational, acceptable expectations with unrealistic, unreasonable, irrational expectations.

THE P52 PROJECT

INTRODUCTION What is Papyrus 52 (P52) Rylands Greek P 457

Papyrus 52 P52

Contents: John 18:31–33, 37–38.

Date: 100 – 150 C.E. (Colins H. Roberts); 100-125 (Comfort and Barrett)

Discovered: Fayum or Oxyrhynchus, Egypt, believed to have been circulated in both areas.

Housing Location: John Rylands Library in Manchester, England.

Physical Features: It is one leaf; 18 cm x 22 cm; 18 lines per page; written in a reformed documentary hand.

Textual Character: P52 is hardly enough to suggest which text type it belongs to. The Alands list it as Category I, or what they call "normal."

P52 is the oldest manuscript of the New Testament known today. It measures 21/2 by 31/2 inches and contains only a few verses of the fourth gospel, John 18:31-33 (recto, the front), 37, and 38 (verso, the back). Bernard P. Grenfell acquired it around 1920, yet it went unnoticed until 1934 when paleographer Colin H. Roberts noticed that it contained the Gospel of John. Roberts had evaluated the fragment, dating it to the beginning of the second century C.E. While other paleographers disagreed, other renowned scholars reached the same conclusion, including Frederic Kenyon, W. Schubart, Harold I. Bell, Adolf Deissmann, Ulrich Wilcken, and W. H. P. Hatch. P52 is especially important because It establishes that the Gospel of John was written in the first century.

We know that P52 was written on a codex and not a roll because it is written on both sides. A codex is a collection of ancient manuscript texts, especially of the Biblical Scriptures, in book form. It is made up of sheets of papyrus or parchment inscribed with handwritten material, which is created by folding a single sheet of standard-sized pages, giving the scribe two leaves or four pages. When we consider the thought of unrolling and using a scroll as opposed to the codex, we can likely think of many advantages of one over the other. The codex has the capacity to contain far more written material; it is much easier to carry and more convenient. Some in the early days of the codex even mentioned these advantages but were slow to move away from the long use of the scroll. The Christians played a major part in the eventual death of the scroll.

While the current paragraph gives a helpful overview of the codex format and its Christian adoption, a deeper codicological analysis can reinforce the argument. Codicological evidence includes not only the use of both recto and verso sides but also microscopic features such as fiber direction, ruling lines, margins, and the number of lines per column. In P52, the vertical alignment of fibers on the recto and the horizontal on the verso clearly demonstrate the standard papyrus sheet layout, further supporting its identity as part of a codex rather than a roll. Moreover, although the fragment is small, the presence of relatively consistent ruling and spacing indicates a controlled and deliberate scribal effort typical of formal literary copying rather than a hastily written document. Including these technical aspects strengthens the claim that P52 is not only part of a codex but also representative of an early Christian scribal tradition with attention to orderly text presentation.

The bolding is mine, which are the letters that can be seen in P52. The square brackets are Comfort and Barrett, which "Indicates conjectural reconstruction of the beginning or ending of a manuscript, or, within the transcriptions, letters or words most likely to have been in the original manuscript." The English is similar to what one would find in an interlinear, which may read a literal rough because it is simply the corresponding literal English word without regard to English grammar and syntax.

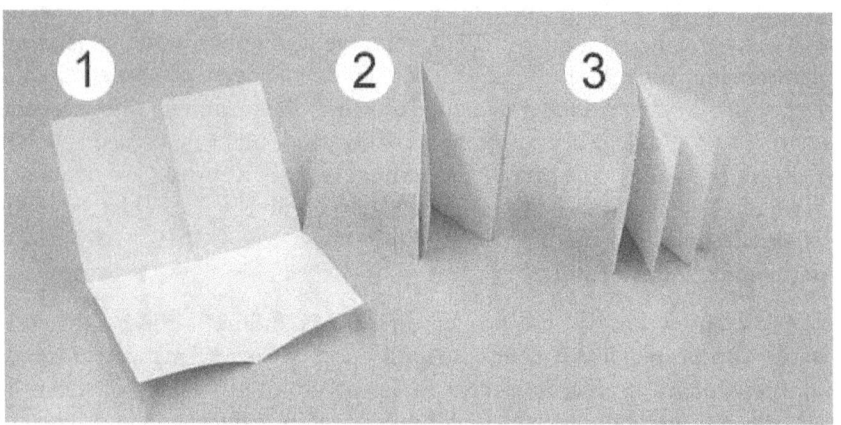

Gospel of John 18:31-33 (recto)
31 ΟΙ ΟΥΔΑΙΙ ΗΜΕ[ΙΝ ΟΥΚ ΕΞΕΣΤΙΝ ΑΠΟΚΤΕΙΝΑΙ
ΟΥΔΕΝΑ 32 ΝΑ Ο ΛΟ[ΓΟΣ ΤΟΥ ΠΛΗΡΩΘΗ ΟΝ ΕΙ
ΠΕΝ ΣΗΜΑΙΝΩ[Ν ΠΟΙΩ ΘΑΝΑΤΩ ΗΜΕΛΛΕΝ ΑΠΟ
ΘΝΗΣΚΕΙΝ 33ΙΣ[ΗΛΘΕΝ ΟΥΝ ΠΑΛΙΝ ΕΙΣ ΤΟ ΠΡΑΙΤΩ
ΡΙΟΝ Ο Π[ΙΛΑΤΟΣ ΚΑΙ ΕΦΩΝΗΣΕΝ ΤΟΝ
ΚΑΙ ΕΙΠ[ΕΝ ΑΥΤΩ ΣΥ ΕΙ Ο ΒΑΣΙΛΕΥΣ ΤΩΝ ΟΥ

THE P52 PROJECT

Δ] ΑΙΩ[Ν

the Jews, "For us it is not permitted to kill
anyone," so that the word of Jesus might be fulfilled, which he sp-
oke signifying what kind of death he was going to
die. Entered therefore again into the Praeto-
rium Pilate and summoned Jesus
and said to him, "Thou art king of the
Jews?"

Gospel of John 18:37-38 (verso)

ΒΑΣΙΛΕΥΣ ΕΙΜΙ ΕΓΩ ΕΙΣ ΤΟ]ΥΤΟ Γ[Ε]ΓΕΝΝΗΜΑΙ
ΚΑΙ (ΕΙΣ ΤΟΥΤΟ) ΕΛΗΛΥΘΑ ΕΙΣ ΤΟΝ ΚΟ]ΣΜΟΝ ΝΑ ΜΑΡΤΥ
ΡΗΣΩ ΤΗ ΑΛΗΘΕΙΑ ΠΑΣ Ο ΩΝ] ΕΚ ΤΗΣ ΑΛΗΘΕ[Ι
ΑΣ ΑΚΟΥΕΙ ΜΟΥ ΤΗΣ ΦΩΝΗΣ] 38 ΛΕΓΕΙ ΑΥΤΩ
Ο ΠΙΛΑΤΟΣ ΤΙ ΕΣΤΙΝ ΑΛΗΘΕΙΑ Κ]ΑΙ ΤΟΥΤΟ
ΕΙΠΩΝ ΠΑΛΙΝ ΕΞΗΛΘΕΝ ΠΡΟΣ] ΤΟΥΣ Ι[ΟΥ
ΔΑΙΟΥΣ ΚΑΙ ΛΕΓΕΙ ΑΥΤΟΙΣ ΕΓΩ ΟΥΔ]ΕΜΙ[ΑΝ
[ΕΥΡΙΣΚΩ ΕΝ ΑΥΤΩ ΑΙΤΙΑΝ

a King I am. For this I have been born
and (for this) I have come into the world so that I would
testify to the truth. Everyone who is of the truth
hears of me my voice." Said to him
Pilate, "What is truth?" and this
having said, again he went out unto the Jews
and said to them, "I find not one
fault in him."

P52 has long been accepted as the earliest extant manuscript of a canonical Greek New Testament text. The original editor, Colin H. Roberts, proposed a date range of 100-150 C.E. We will take an in-depth look at his findings in Chapter. The following paleographers and papyrologists agree with Roberts' dating of P52.

Paleographers and Textual Scholars Date P52 Early

- 100-150 C. H. Roberts
- 100-150 Sir Frederic G. Kenyon
- 100-150 W. Schubart
- 100-150 Sir Harold I. Bell
- 100-150 Adolf Deissmann
- 100-150 E. G. Turner (cautiously)
- 100-150 Ulrich Wilken

- 100-150 W. H. P. Hatch
- 100-150 Daniel B. Wallace
- 100-125: Philip W. Comfort
- 100-150 Bruce M. Metzger
- 125-175 Kurt and Barbara Aland
- 125-175 Pasquale Orsini
- 125-175 Willy Clarysse
- 170 C.E. Andreas Schmidt

Other More Recent Textual Scholars Date P52

- 100-225 Brent Nongbri
- 81–292 Don Barker
- 200-300 Michael Gronewald

However, this general agreement would not hold, and scholars' consensus would come to an end. Recently, Pasquale Orsini (Italian paleographer, librarian, and Professor) and Willy Clarysse sought to revisit the dating of the Greek New Testament papyri before the fourth century, and according to their proposal, P52 dates to 125-175 C.E. Nevertheless, we have a few scholars who have come to different conclusions. Andreas Schmidt is still close to Roberts' range with his dating P52 to 170 C.E. It is Brent Nongbri with the date (100-225 C.E.), Don Barker with the date of 81–292 C.E., and Michael Gronewald with 200-300 C.E. who seem to want to overturn the dating of small fragments solely on paleographic evidence. Just how weighty is this new evidence? Brent Nongbri writes, "What emerges from this survey is nothing surprising to papyrologists: paleography is not the most effective method for dating texts, particularly those written in a literary hand." We will take this up later in Chapter 3. The approach to this book is to give you, the reader, the evidence presented by each paleographer, papyrologist, or textual scholar in their chapter, which will also include this author's analysis of their analysis. Also, P. Egerton 2 will have its chapter as it plays a major role in the dating and redating of P52. Finally, I will close the book with a concluding chapter with my overall observation of whether a handful of new textual scholars, paleographers, and papyrologists have overthrown the work of numerous world-renowned scholars. As is true in most criminal court cases, you hear only one side of the evidence and quickly jump to a verdict. Then, the other side gets up and presents their evidence, and you now change your view. It is best here to pay attention to all the evidence all of the way through before making up your mind. I know that seems simple, but it needed to be said.

THE P52 PROJECT
CHAPTER 1 P. Egerton 2

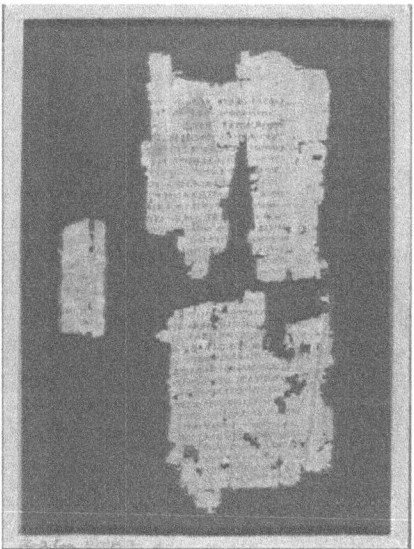

Really, for Christians, there should be no surprise that there have been papyrus manuscripts discovered that contain the sayings of Jesus that are not exactly the same as that of our canonical Gospels. The apostle John himself wrote in 98 C.E. "And there are also many other things which Jesus did, which if they were written one by one, I suppose that even the world itself would not contain the books that would be written." (John 21:25) Luke also infers this in his Gospel introduction when he writes, "Inasmuch as many have undertaken to compile an account of the things accomplished among us, ... it seemed good to me also, having followed all things accurately from the beginning, to write an orderly account for you ..." – Luke 1:1-3.

At Oxyrhynchus, Egypt, in 1897, papyrologists Grenfell and Hunt discovered from a rubbish mound a single damaged papyrus leaf. It was determined that it was from a Greek codex of the third century [200-300] containing supposed sayings of Jesus. The fragment, like many others, is commonly referred to as Oxyrhynchus Papyrus based on the location of the discovery that is now online (e.g., https://bit.ly/2UQ1zUT). An English translation reads:

"Jesus saith, 'Except ye fast to the world, ye shall in no wise find the kingdom of God; and except you make the sabbath a real sabbath, ye shall not see the Father.' Jesus saith, 'I stood in the midst of the world, and in the flesh was I seen of them, and I found all men drunken, and none found I athirst among them, and my soul grieveth over the sons of men, because they are blind in their heart, and see not.' Jesus saith, 'A prophet is not acceptable in his own country, neither doth a physician work cures upon them that know him.' Jesus saith, 'A city built upon the top of a high hill and established, can neither fall nor be hid.'"

We notice that the first supposed two sayings of Jesus are extra-biblical. In other words, there is no connection to the canonical Gospels. Numerous scholars have claimed that these are some of the "many other things" to which John refers to in John 21:25, which were never recorded in the canonical Bible. Now, if we look at the saying, part of which says, "A prophet is not acceptable in his own country," it is comparable to Matthew 13:57. However, the rest of it is a part of the "many other things" to which John may have been referring. The fourth saying is quite similar to Matthew 5:14.

Yet another discovery of "sayings" came to light in 1934 when the British Museum, London, obtained a number of papyri fragments from a dealer. Within these fragments were some of an 'unknown life of Jesus,' which was written in a hand that has been dated to about 150 C.E. In 1935, H. I. Bell and T. C. Skeat, who were librarians at the British Museum, working as Assistant Keepers of the manuscripts, published the photostats of the three leaves that had been discovered. As it happened, these were part of an old Greek codex that had originated in Egypt. These fragmentary pages are now known as "Egerton Papyrus 2."

Together they comprise one of the oldest surviving witnesses to any gospel or any codex. The British Museum lost no time in publishing the text: acquired in the summer of 1934, it was in print in 1935. It has also been called the Unknown Gospel, as no ancient source refers to it, in addition to being entirely unknown before its publication. The fragmentary manuscript forms part of the Egerton Collection in the British Library. A fourth fragment of the same manuscript has since been identified in the papyrus collection of the University of Cologne.

The surviving fragments include four stories: (1) a controversy similar to John 5:39-47 and 10:31-39; (2) curing a leper similar to Matt 8:1-4, Mark 1:40-45, Luke 5:12-16 and Luke 17:11-14; (3) a controversy about paying tribute to Caesar analogous to Matt 22:15-22, Mark 12:13-17, Luke 20:20-26; and (4) an incomplete account of a miracle on the Jordan River bank, perhaps carried out to illustrate the parable about seeds growing miraculously. The latter story has no equivalent in the canonical Gospels:

THE P52 PROJECT

Jesus walked and stood on the bank of the Jordan river; he reached out his right hand, and filled it.... And he sowed it on the... And then...water...and...before their eyes; and it brought forth fruit...many...for joy...

Image Egerton Papyrus 2 (150 C.E.) Verso θC (Theos)

The Nomina Sacra

This Greek text, especially with the early dating of 150 C.E., evidences a scribal custom that had recently developed. The scribes used suspensions (IH XP. Ἰησοῦς Χριστός [Jesus Christ]) or contractions (ΘΣ, Θεός, Theos, God), to which he would place a bar over the entire name (), for sacred names and words (nomina sacra). Nomina Sacra (singular: nomen sacrum from Latin sacred name): In early Christian scribal practices (how early we cannot know), several frequently occurring divine names or titles were abbreviated within the Greek manuscripts. The very earliest copyists used a special form for the divine names: kurios (Lord), Iēsous (Jesus), Christos (Christ), theos (God), and pneuma (Spirit). In time, the list grew to fifteen names or words.

$$\overline{IC}, \overline{XC}, \overline{YC}, \overline{\Pi NA}, \overline{K\Sigma}$$

Image Jesus, Christ, Son, Spirit, Lord

It should be noted that "the nomina sacra for Lord, Jesus, Christ, God, and Spirit are present in all extant second-century New Testament manuscripts where one or more of these nomina sacra are extant. The following second-century manuscripts that clearly show these nomina sacra are as follows:

- P4+P64+P67—Matthew, Luke

- P32—Titus
- P46—Paul's Epistles
- P66—John
- P75—Luke, John
- P90—John"

This practice by the Christian scribes followed the custom of the Jewish scribes and their rendering of the Tetragrammaton or sacred name יהוה [JHVH] in Greek by the words kyrios ("Lord") without the definite article and theos ("God") with only the first and last letters written and a stroke above them. P4+P64+P67 dates to (150-175 C.E.), P32 dates to (150-200 C.E.), P46 dates to 150 C.E.), P66 dates to about (150 C.E.), P75 dates to about (175 C.E.), and P90 dates to (150-200 C.E.). This means that the nomina sacra for Lord, Jesus, Christ, God, and Spirit are standard by 150 C.E. This would suggest that, after the death of the last apostle John died in about 100 C.E., more than just division started to set in, as the apostles had really served as a restraint against the great apostasy that was about to come. Now, this little excursion into an area that might seem totally unrelated is just to say we cannot know what the authors penned in their autographs, nor the first generation of copyists, based on mid-late second-century manuscripts. Why? The phenomena of the standardization of the nomina sacra only need about fifty years to take place. Of course, John wrote his Gospels, three letters, and the book of Revelation between 96-98 C.E., so we can say that his writings would have been closest. The other Bible books were all authored before 70 C.E.

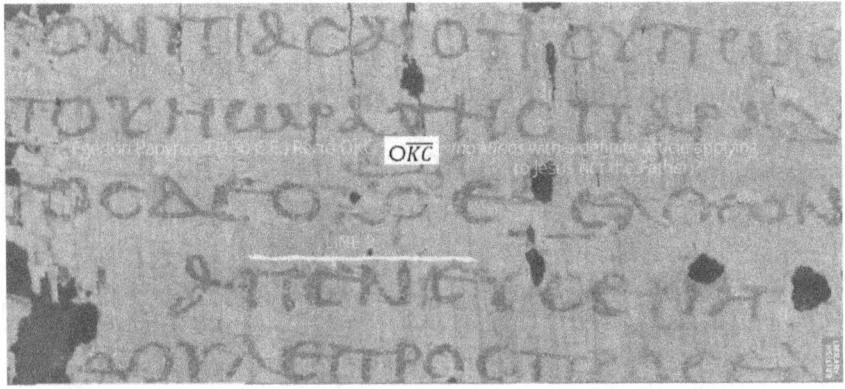

Image Egerton Papyrus 2 Recto OKC

Again, the first four nominal sacra were ('Jesus,' 'God,' 'Lord,' and 'Christ') in the earliest extant manuscripts that we have. It is possible that the personal name of the Father, Jehovah, could be designated in the Greek as and were the first attempts at the nomina sacra. The Christian scribes soon thereafter expanded the list of abbreviations that included the following: ho kyrios (the Lord) with a definite article applying to Jesus, not the Father? Followed by (Iesous, Jesus). Was the initial attempt with the title for the father replacing the Tetragrammaton or sacred name יהוה in Greek without the definite article? Also,, the title for the father replacing the Tetragrammaton or sacred name יהוה in Greek? In addition, we have (patera, father) and (Moÿses, Moses). It is undoubtedly an anomaly that we find Moses' name abbreviated by suspension (the first two letters) here in P. Egerton 2, similar to how Jesus' name is treated. Comfort writes, "Scattered across the pages of nearly every extant Greek New Testament manuscript can be seen the following nomina sacra." (Encountering the Manuscripts, 2005, 199). The contraction or suspended word would have a bar over it.

ΚΣ for κυριος (Kurios) = Lord
ΙΗ or ΙΗΣ for ιησους (Iēsous) = Jesus
ΧΡ or ΧΣ or ΧΡΣ for χριστος (Christos) = Christ
ΘΣ for θεος (theos) = God
ΠΝΑ for πνευμα (pneuma) = Spirit

George Howard argues that κς (κύριος) and θς (θεός) were the initial nomina sacra, created by non-Jewish Christian scribes who "found no traditional reasons to preserve the Tetragrammaton" in copies of the Septuagint. Larry W. Hurtado, following Colin Roberts, rejects that claim in favor of the theory that the first was ιη (Ἰησοῦς), as suggested in the Epistle of Barnabas, followed by the analogous χρ (Χριστός), and later by κς and θς, at about the time when the contracted forms ις and χς were adopted for the first two. It is possible that the personal name of the Father, Jehovah, could be designated in the Greek as κς (κύριος) and θς (θεός) and were the first attempts at the nomina sacra. Comfort writes,

> The nomina sacra are also present in Greek Old Testament manuscripts and other Christian writings produced by Christians. This includes several second-century manuscripts noted below:
>
> P. Chester Beatty VI, Numbers, Deuteronomy
> P. Baden 4.56 (P. Heidelberg inv. 8), Exodus and Deuteronomy
> P. Antinoopolis 7, Psalms
> PSI 921, Psalms
> P. Oxyrhynchus 1074, Exodus

P. Chester Beatty Papyrus VIII, Jeremiah
P. Chester Beatty Papyrus IX, Ezekiel, Daniel, Esther

Other Christian writings also use nomina sacra:

P. Geneva 253, Christian homily
P. Egerton 2, Unknown Gospel
P. Oxyrhynchus 405, fragment of Irenaeus
P. Oxyrhynchus 406, Christian homily

One of the main reasons we know that the Old Testament manuscripts are Christian manuscripts and not Jewish is the presence of nomina sacra in the text. Significantly, not one copy of the Greek Old Testament found at Qumran has these nomina sacra because this was a Jewish, not a Christian community. Jews never wrote nomina sacra the way Christians did; the Jews did things differently for one divine name and one divine name only: Yahweh. Jewish scribes would frequently write this in its Hebrew contracted form (even in paleo-Hebrew letters) and then continue on with the Greek text. Christians used **κυριος** (*kurios* = Lord) in place of Yahweh (YHWH) and wrote it in nomen sacrum form. Many Greek Old Testament manuscripts produced by Christians display this nomen sacrum. This can be seen in all six second-century Greek Old Testament manuscripts noted above.[1]

Image Egerton Papyrus 2 (150 C.E.) Verso Moses & Father

Take a look at the image below at "1 verso" and note in line 12, in line 13 and in line 16. Next, look at "1 recto" and note in line 9 and in line 12. However, we do not have Kyrios without the definite article, which would apply to the Father in the fragments. Really, we can say that it is likely that

---

[1] Philip Comfort, *Encountering the Manuscripts: An Introduction to New Testament Paleography & Textual Criticism* (Nashville, TN: Broadman & Holman, 2005), 202.

150 C.E. was entering the time of standardization of the nomina sacra that would grow in sacred names and words.

Sir Frederic Kenyon was a British palaeographer and biblical and classical scholar, commented on these fragments. "They contain four episodes in the life of our Lord, told quite simply, and therefore unlike the exaggerated and fanciful style of later apocryphal gospels, and in language showing strong affinities, sometimes with the Synoptic Gospels (Matthew, Mark, and Luke) and sometimes with the Fourth Gospel (John). The exact wording is often left doubtful by the mutilation of the papyrus, but the main drift of three out of the four episodes is clear." The superior verse below provided by Edward D. Andrews into Bell and Skeat's translation is his notes indicating those portions paralleled in the Biblical accounts.)

Egerton Gospel Translation

The Unknown Gospel Egerton Papyrus 2 + Cologne Papyrus 255 Fragment 1: Verso (?)

... ? And Jesus said] unto the lawyers, [? Punish] every wrongdoer and transgessor, and not me;..... And turning to the rulers of the people he spake this saying, Search the scriptures, in which ye think that ye have life; these are they which bear witness of me. [John 5:39.] Think not that I came to accuse you to my Father; there is one that accuseth you, even Moses, on whom ye have set your hope. [John 5:45] And when they said, We know well that God spake unto Moses, but as for thee, we know not whence thou art, [John 9:29] Jesus answered and said unto them, Now is your unbelief accused ...

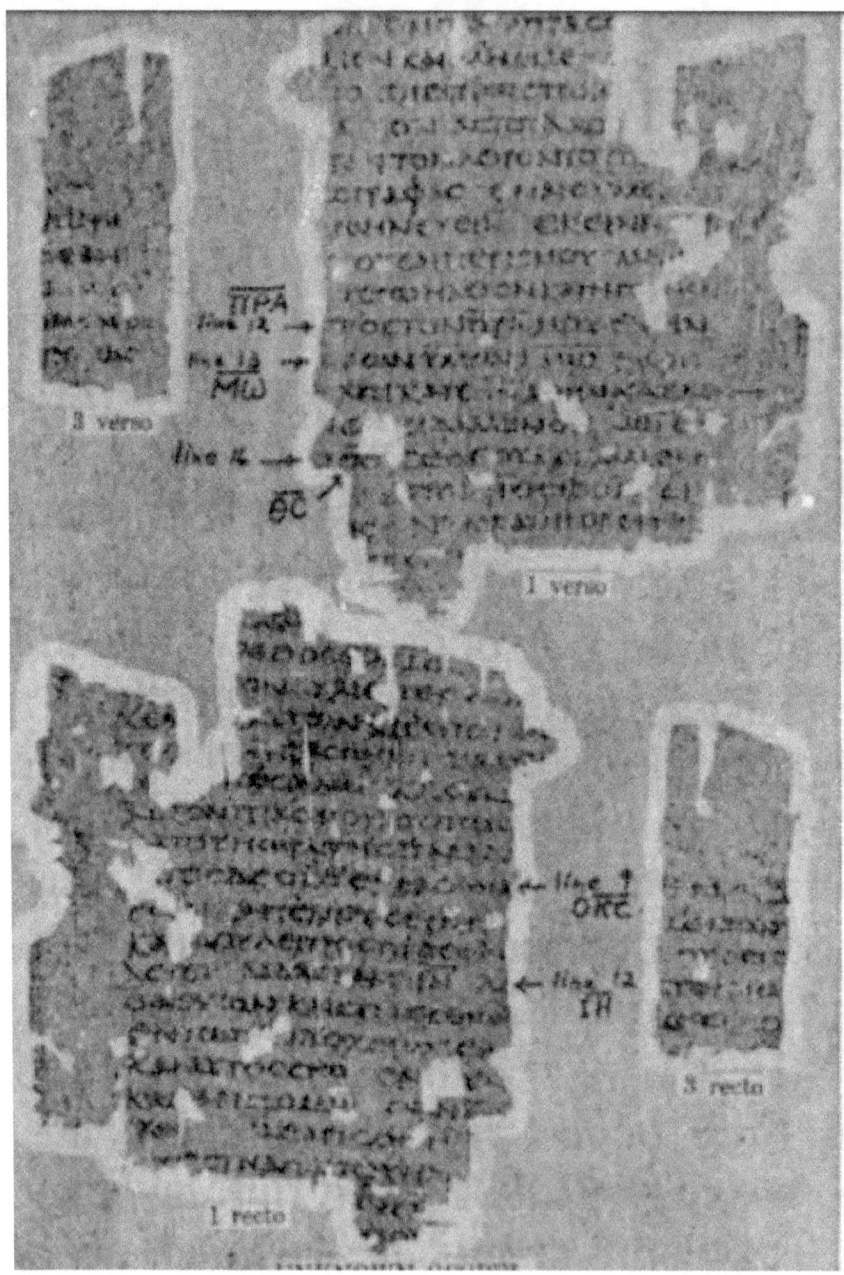

Fragment 1: Recto (?)

... ? they gave counsel to] the multitude to [? carry the] stones together and stone him. [John 8:59; 10:31] And the rulers sought to lay their hands on him that they might take him and [? hand him over] to the multitude; and they could not take him, because the hour of his betrayal was not yet come. [John 7:30] But he himself, even the Lord, going out through the midst of them, departed from them. [Luke 4:30] And behold, there cometh unto him a leper and saith, Master Jesus, journeying with lepers and eating with them in the inn I myself also became a leper. If therefore thou wilt, I am made clean. The Lord then said unto him, I will; be thou made clean. And straightway the leprosy departed from him. [And the Lord said unto him], Go [and shew thyself] unto the [priests...

Fragment 2: Recto (?)

... coming unto him began to tempt him with a question, saying, Master Jesus, we know that thou art come from God, [John 3:2; Matt. 22:16] for the things which thou doest testify above all the prophets. [John 10:25] Tell us therefore: Is it lawful [? to render] unto kings that which pertaineth unto their rule? [Shall we render unto them], or not? [Matt. 22:17] But Jesus, knowing their thought, [Matt. 9:4] being moved with indignation, said unto them, Why call ye me with your mouth Master, when ye hear not what I say? [Luke 6:46] Well did Isaiah prophesy of you, saying, This people honour me with their lips, but their heart is far from me. In vain do they worship me, [teaching as their doctrines the] precepts [of men] [Matt. 15:7-9] ...

Fragment 2: Verso (?)

... shut up... in... place... its weight unweighed? And when they were perplexed at his strange question, Jesus, as he walked, stood still on the edge of the river Jordan, and stretching forth his right hand he... and sprinkled it upon the... And then... water that had been sprinkled... before them and sent forth fruit... Translation reprinted from: H.I. Bell and T.C. Skeat, Fragments of an Unknown Gospel and Other Early Christian Papyri (London: Oxford University Press, 1935).

Dating the Egerton Gospel

Like P52, the P. Egerton Gospel 2 manuscript is dated on paleography grounds alone. When the Egerton fragments were first published, they too were dated to about 150 C.E.; similar to Papyrus Rylands Gk 457 (P52), which put in on the same footing with P52 (found in Egypt) in dispelling the notion the Gospel of John had been authored around 150-170 C.E., as P52 is a copy of the Gospel of John and P. Egerton 2 was using John's Gospel as a basis for his document. In 1987 an additional papyrus fragment of the

Egerton Gospel was discovered in the University of Cologne collection (Papyrus Köln 255). It was discovered that it fit on the bottom of one of the papyrus pages at the British Library. When inspected, it was discovered that there was a hooked apostrophe in between two consonants gamma and kappa (aneneg'kon). This became a standard practice among the scribes after 200 C.E. (third century); and for this reason alone, the date of P. Egerton 2 was revised among some (e.g., Michael Gronewald, Brent Nongbri, and A. Schmidt) to no earlier than 200 C.E. This discovery of the hooked apostrophe and the words of papyrologist Eric Turner placed the manuscript to 200 C.E. along with the Bodmer Papyri P66. What Turner actually said was: "In the first decade of iii ad this practice [of placing an apostrophe between two consonants] suddenly becomes extremely common and then persists." We note that Turner said it was until the third century A.D. and later that "this practice" became "extremely common" and then "persists." He did not say that it did not exist before the start of the third century because he knew as well as we know today, "this practice" was developing in the second century. Turner himself then gives three examples: (Αγ'χωριμφις in BGU iii 715.5 dating to A.D. 101) and (P.Petaus 86.11 dating to A.D. 184/85; SB XIV 11342.11 dating to A.D. 193).

Comfort writes,

> I would argue that the previously assigned date of such manuscripts was given by many scholars according to their observations of several paleographic features. Thus, the presence of this particular feature (the hook or apostrophe between double consonants) determines an earlier date for its emergence, not the other way around. Thus, the Egerton Gospel, dated by many to ca. 150, should still stand, and so should the date for P52 (as early second century). Another way to come at this is to look at P66, dated by several scholars to ca. 150 (see discussion below). Turner, however, would date P66 later (early third) largely because of the presence of the hook between double consonants. What I would say is that the predominant dating of P66 (i.e., the dating assigned by most scholars) predetermines the date for this particular feature. Furthermore, there are other manuscripts dated prior to AD 200 that exhibit the apostrophe or hook between double consonants:
>
> 1. BGU iii 715.5 (AD 101)
>
> Αγ'χωριμφις
>
> 2. P. Petaus 86 (= P. Michigan 6871) (AD 185)
>
> Αγ'γων
>
> 3. SPP xxii 3.22 (second century)

> Απυγ´χεως
>
> 4. P. Berol. 9570 + P. Rylands 60 (dated by the editors of the *editio princeps* to ca. 200, dated by Cavallo to ca. 50)
>
> Φαλαγ´γας[2]

However, this author and others would date P66 to c. 150 A.D.

All throughout the Christian Church in its early centuries New Testament texts displayed the nomina sacra. Special notice was given to "Lord," "Jesus," "Christ," "God," and "Spirit." Whether we accept Hurtado's hypothesis as to the how and why of the rise of the nomina sacra, or we go with other suggestions, we cannot make the connection back to the originals 27 New Testament manuscripts, or the first generation of copyists. Some would suggest Lord (κυριος, kurios), written as ΚΣ was first in the line of the nomina sacra (as Philip Comfort would suggest), or Jesus (ιησους, Iēsous), written as IH (as Larry Hurtado suggests). I would tend to agree with Comfort, and for the same reason, he offers as well.

It would seem to this author; the best suggestion is the desire of the second century C.E. Christianity and Pharisaic Judaism to separate themselves from each other. For example, you have Judaism abandoning the Greek translation of the Old Testament, the Septuagint, even though they were espousing it to be inspired just a few decades earlier. Why? The Christians had adopted the Septuagint as their evangelism tool because the de facto language of the Roman Empire was Koine Greek.

Here we can see second-century Christianity in their move to distance themselves from Judaism by not adopting the same practice, even though it is likely that many of the Christian copyists were Jewish. In other words, "a scribe or scribes (whether Jewish Christian or Gentile Christian) created a nomen sacrum form for kurios (Lord), reflecting knowledge of and purposeful distinction from the Hebrew Tetragrammaton, YHWH." At the beginning of the second century C.E., there were a number of things beginning to take place. (1) Judaism wanted to separate itself from Christianity. (2) Christianity wanted to distance itself from Judaism. (3) The Jews were starting to replace the Tetragrammaton (יהוה, JHVH) with 'Adhonai´ (Lord), as they felt the divine name was too sacred to pronounce. (4) Christians began the transition of Lord (κυριος, kurios), written as ΚΣ being first in the line of the nomina sacra that was to come. (5) The Jews had produced the Greek Septuagint and translation of the Hebrew Old

---

[2] Philip Comfort, *Encountering the Manuscripts: An Introduction to New Testament Paleography & Textual Criticism* (Nashville, TN: Broadman & Holman, 2005), 108–109.

Testament Scriptures between 280-150 B.C.E. They had come to accept the Septuagint as inspired until the Christians began to favor the translation as well. The Jews returned to the Hebrew Old Testament because Christians had taken the Greek Septuagint as an apologetic tool to defend Jesus as the long-awaited Messiah.

CHAPTER 2 Paleography: The Criteria Used for Dating Ancient Manuscripts

Paleography is the study of ancient handwriting and manuscripts. The discipline includes the practices of deciphering, reading, and dating historical manuscripts and the cultural context of writing, including the methods with which writing and books were produced and the history of scriptoria.

Greek Paleography and Its Beginnings

Bernard de Montfaucon (1655-1741), a French Benedictine monk, who established the new discipline of paleography, laid the groundwork for the meticulous study of Greek manuscripts. He is also viewed as the originator of modern archaeology. As time passed, other scholars would make their contributions, as well. Tischendorf would comb Europe and its libraries, cataloging, and discovering manuscripts along the way. During several trips to the Middle East, he had the opportunity to investigate several hundred other manuscripts. In the end, he would publish his findings in numerous critical editions of the Greek text, but his eighth (1869-72), to this day, is used by textual scholars as a colossal thesaurus of variant readings.

The 20th century saw an explosion of tools that have served as helps to paleographers. We have the Schoenberg Database of Manuscripts (SDBM), the Marcel Richard list of some 900 catalogs that describe 55,000 Greek manuscripts, The Center for the Study of New Testament Manuscripts, POxy: Oxyrhynchus Online, and the Institute for New Testament Textual Criticism in Münster, Germany. All of these are found on the internet, giving access to anyone who owns a computer. This storehouse of information and technology has proved to be a tremendous help to the textual scholar, the paleographer, and papyrologists. They have done the job of helping them determine a manuscript's age much easier and more precisely.

How do Paleographers Date Manuscripts?

Imagine that we are paleographers rummaging through the library of an old monastery, one that dates to the third century C.E. As we carefully move books aside, we discover that there are other loose pages within one of the books on the shelf. As we pull out the pages, we have discovered what looks to be an ancient uncial Greek document. As we continue to work our way through the books, looking for more pages, we are wondering about the age of this document. To our delight, the last page provides a clue that would establish the date within 50 years. It was not the same manuscript, but it was the same hand, the same style, the same handwriting, the same punctuation, as well as other features that would establish this as the same person who made the other Biblical manuscript. However, this manuscript has a date on it.

Sadly, it was not a practice of scribes to place dates in their literary manuscripts after they had completed them. Thus, the textual scholar must compare other documents that have secured dates, both Biblical literary and non-Biblical literary and documentary texts, to then decide from an investigation of the handwriting, punctuation, abbreviations, letter and line spacing, and the like. What we may have at times is a literary text on one side of the page, and a documentary text on the other side, making it easier to establish the date of the literary text.

Handwriting Investigation

How do textual scholars know that the manuscript dates to the second, third, or fourth century C.E., or any other century? If we were to pull any book from our bookshelf and turn a few pages in it, we would normally find the date of publication on the copyright page. If we bought a used book that was missing the copyright page, we would have no idea when it was published. It is only because of modern technology that we could date the book. Extant ancient literary manuscripts hardly ever had dates on them.

However, ancient documentary manuscripts do, which is crucial in our ability to date the undated literary manuscripts.

By employing the art and science of paleography, we can arrive at an approximate date when the manuscript was written. Terminus post quem ("limit after which") and terminus ante quem ("limit before which") specify the known limits of dating a manuscript. A terminus post quem is the earliest time the manuscript could have been written, and a terminus ante quem is the latest time the manuscript could have been written.

Paleographers could be viewed as manuscript detectives; through their knowledge of the writing of ancient texts, the forms, and styles, we get a reasonably close idea of when a manuscript was copied. For example, when looking at our modern languages today, we can see that there are subtle changes within every generation or two. This holds true of ancient languages as well. Through painstaking comparison of hundreds of small features within an ancient manuscript, a paleographer can provide us with a date that is usually correct to plus or minus 25 to 50 years. Such features can distinguish certain periods as the amount of punctuation within a manuscript, abbreviations, and the amount of spacing between letters or words. There are certain documents such as receipts, letters, leases, and petitions that do contain dates. It is these that have formed a library of letters with the styles that go into making each letter during different time periods.

Before we look at the dating saga of P52, we need to take a deeper dive into what goes into what criteria will be used in determining the date of P52. Many clues go into dating a manuscript. The foremost is the writing style of the copyist himself, and styles always change over time. The scribes of P52 and P. Egerton 2 are practiced scribes (he has skills at making documentary manuscripts but can produce a literary document if called on to do so), not a professional scribe. Thus, if a given manuscript uses an angular hand of the early third century C.E., it is likely from the early third century C.E. As we look at the clues for dating P52, we hope to show how to use them. In addition, if we show a manuscript image, we will highlight how it is to be used. We will make statements like, "observe the form of the letter _____. This is common of second-century usage." Such help is needed if some readers who have limited knowledge of the subject are to come to the same conclusions. And this book does not just supply them. We are going to look at three different criteria that can be used in dating manuscripts but may not necessarily be used in our discussion of P52: Archaeological Evidence, Codicology, and Comparative Paleography.

Archaeological evidence can be used in dating manuscripts with no dates. However, in almost all cases, archaeology really does not play a role in dating the Greek New Testament papyri. An example where it can be used would be P4+P64+P67, as it "cannot be dated later than AD 200 because it was placed in strips (perhaps as binding) for a third-century codex of Philo. Some length of time must be allowed for a well-written codex to have been used to such an extent that it was torn up and used as binding." Comfort writes, "The manuscript P4 figures significantly in assigning a date because we know about its provenance. It had been used for padding in a codex of Philo's treatises that was hidden in a house in Coptos to avoid being confiscated during the persecution of A.D. 292 or 303 when Coptos was besieged and sacked by Diocletian. The Philo codex is itself a third-century manuscript that could be dated 25–50 years prior to the time it was put in hiding. Thus, the Philo codex can be dated at least to about A.D. 250. The owner of the Gospel codex was probably a Christian and, therefore, would have valued the Gospels. He would not have used a newly copied Gospel as stuffing for Philo's treatises, so this Gospel codex must have been well used and well worn. In fact, it must have been a discarded copy replaced by another codex. Thus, P4 may have been made as early as a hundred years prior to A.D. 250, if not earlier. So we are fairly certain of at least a late-second-century date, but this does not preclude an earlier date, because the codex may have been in use more than a hundred years before it was discarded."

Codicology (from codex) is the study of codices, manuscript books written on papyrus, parchment, or paper. It has been referred to as "the archaeology of the book." It is "the science of the codex." It deals with how the codices were put together, the materials used, techniques used, how the text was laid out, and even their binding. "And since Paul himself made mention of codices, it stands to reason that Paul's epistles were the first to be collected into codex form." The codex came into use by the Christians in the first century and was popularized by the Christians in the second century.

Christian Book Production and the Rise of the Codex in the Second Century

By the second century C.E., a distinct trend was emerging among Christian communities: the preferential use of the **codex** format over the traditional scroll. While Roman and Jewish cultures largely retained the scroll for literary texts, Christians gravitated toward the codex with such consistency that it became a defining feature of early Christian manuscript culture. This widespread adoption was not merely a matter of convenience but reflected theological, evangelistic, and practical motivations unique to the Christian movement.

Codices allowed for **more compact storage**, **easier transport**, and **rapid reference**—features that were ideal for missionary activity, public reading, and theological instruction. Unlike the scroll, which could only be read in sequence, the codex enabled Christians to flip quickly between texts, especially beneficial when using multiple Old Testament passages to support messianic claims or responding to false teachings. Furthermore, early Christian writings—such as the Gospels and Paul's epistles—were often grouped together in collections, and the codex format provided a way to bind these materials into a unified volume. This facilitated the **formation and dissemination of a Christian canon**, long before canon lists were formalized.

Scholarly analysis of surviving papyri confirms this trend. According to statistics compiled by Larry W. Hurtado and others, over 95% of extant Christian manuscripts from the second and third centuries are in codex form. In contrast, the wider Greco-Roman literary culture continued using scrolls well into the third and fourth centuries. This discrepancy underscores that the Christian adoption of the codex was not simply a reflection of broader cultural shifts—it was a **conscious and early development** within the Christian scribal tradition.

The **earliest Christian manuscripts** we possess—such as P52 (John), P46 (Paul's epistles), P66 (John), and P75 (Luke and John)—are all written in codex format. This aligns with what we see in P52: a single leaf from a codex, written on both recto and verso, indicating a deliberate choice of form. While the fragment itself is small, its format places it squarely within the well-documented trend of second-century Christian codex usage.

The uniformity of codex use across geographically diverse Christian communities (e.g., Egypt, Syria, Asia Minor) suggests this was not merely regional or coincidental. Early Christian preference for the codex, combined with the paleographic style of P52, supports the conclusion that P52 was produced by a Christian scribe as part of an organized manuscript culture that prioritized the codex for both theological and functional reasons. The early date of P52 is thus not an anomaly—it fits within the **larger picture of second-century Christian book production**, helping to affirm the traditional dating of 100–150 C.E.

Figure 1 P52 Recto Side   Figure 2 P52 Verso Side

Comparative paleography is exactly as it sounds, comparing a literary manuscript that has no dating with a documentary manuscript that does have a date. The problem paleographers have long faced is that most manuscript books do not contain dates. Therefore, the strongest means for arriving at a date for biblical manuscripts, which are literary documents is to compare them with documentary texts, that is, manuscripts that have documentary information, such as dates. When we look at a sheet from a codex, the recto and verso are correspondingly the "front" and "back" sides of that codex sheet. On this Comfort writes,

> If a literary text has been written on the recto (the best and therefore the primary side of a papyrus or parchment leaf) and a dated documentary work has been written on the verso, the date of the documentary text provides the *terminus ante quem* (latest possible date) because the documentary text will be later. For example, a literary text on the recto, having a documentary text dated AD 150 on the verso, indicates that the literary text must be dated earlier than AD 150. We cannot be sure how much earlier, but the length of time could be quite substantial, perhaps as long as fifty to one hundred years because a literary text would normally have been used (or shelved) for a long period prior to being relegated to

documentary use. As will be discussed below, one sumptuous literary text in the Heroninos collection, P. Rylands 16 (an unknown Comedy), was not relegated to documentary use (on the verso) for well over fifty to seventy-five, perhaps even one hundred years.

Fortunately, several manuscripts have been discovered that have a literary text on the recto and a dated documentary text on the verso. These manuscripts have enabled paleographers to establish the *terminus ante quem* (latest possible date) for the literary texts. As a rule of thumb, paleographers will usually subtract twenty-five to fifty years from the *terminus ante quem* when dating the literary text, for it is conjectured that the literary text (on the recto) must have been well used and well worn before being relegated to documentary use. Such literary texts with relatively certain dates provide models for comparative paleography.

If a literary text has been written on the verso of a documentary text (such as a letter or an official edict), which provides a date, then the documentary text provides the *terminus post quem* (the earliest possible date) for the literary text. For example, a date of AD 150 for a documentary text on the recto, with a literary text on the verso, means that the literary text cannot be dated earlier than AD 150. The length of time between the reuse of a documentary text for literary purposes would normally be shorter, probably around five to fifteen years at most inasmuch as the user would not have valued the document highly if he or she quickly put it to literary use. Let us take, for example, the Christian Psalms fragment, PSI 921 (Psalm 77:1–18). This is a fragment of Psalms written on the verso of a roll containing a bank register (on the recto) dated in AD 143/144. As such, it is quite likely that the Psalms portion should be dated anywhere between AD 155 and 170 (see comments below on this specific manuscript). Another example is P. Michigan 130, the Shepherd of Hermas. This manuscript, containing "The Mandates" of *The Shepherd*, was written on the verso of a scroll; the recto contains a document that can be dated to the reign of Marcus Aurelius (AD 161–180). Thus, it stands to reason that P. Michigan 130 could be dated AD 180–200.

The primary means of dating a New Testament manuscript, as an undated literary text, is by doing a comparative analysis with the handwriting of other dated documentary texts. The second method is to do a comparative analysis with literary manuscripts having a date based on the association with a documentary text on the recto or verso.[3]

---

[3] Philip Wesley Comfort and David P. Barrett, *The Text of the Earliest New Testament Greek Manuscripts* (Grand Rapids, MI: Kregel Academics, 2019), Vol. II, 282-3.

Clues from Handwriting

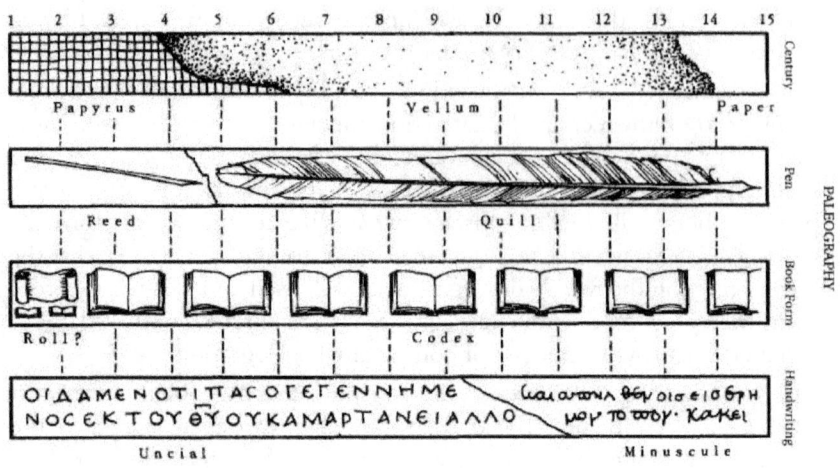

Image Harold Greenlee, Introduction to New Testament Textual Criticism, (p. 23)

Paleographers divide up ancient Greek handwriting into two fundamental categories: book hand, which is rustic capitals. It was meant for legibility and was often used in copying books, official documents, letters, and writings of everyday life. Then, there was cursive, which was initially simplified capital writing, a form of running or flowing writing used in nonliterary personal and business documents. The scribes also used numerous styles of letters, such as capitals, uncials (a form of capitals), cursives, and minuscules. There was one form of the book hand, uncial writing, which was used from the fourth century B.C.E. up until the eighth or ninth century, fading out gradually in the eleventh century C.E. Minuscule writing was a small form of the book hand, which was starting to be used from the ninth to the tenth century C.E. up until the middle of the fifteenth century when Johannes Gutenberg invented printing in 1455. The minuscule script had the advantage of being able to be written more rapidly and taking up less space, which saved money, time, and parchment.

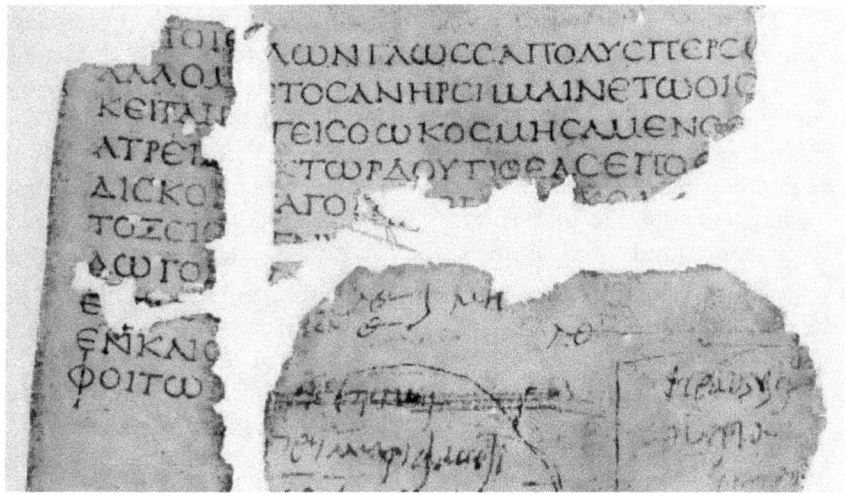

Image P.Oxyrhunchus-XX-Homer-Book-II-SS-1024x578 - Oxyrhynchus papyri Homer's Iliad

Handwriting on Papyrus

The New Testament paleographer is dealing with four different handwriting styles in early Christianity: The Roman Uncial, the Biblical Uncial, the Decorated Rounded Uncial, and the Severe (or Slanted) style. It is no easy task to distinguish them apart from each other or determine where one ends, and the other begins, as there is a great deal of crossover. Even so, each style has its common features, and there is a timeline for the development of these features of a given style, a period of popularity, and the petering out of that style.

The Roman Uncial

Image Papyrus 46 (P46) Date: 150 C.E. Physical Features: In the original form, it would have had 52 folios, which equals 104 leaves, 208 pages. However, in its current condition, 9 folios are missing. It is 15 cm × 27 cm, with 25–31 lines per page, a single column of 26 – 32 lines of text per page. Its pagination is 1 – 199. P46 was written by a professional scribe.

The papyri of the Roman period, unlike the Ptolemaic period that ended about 30 B.CE., are far more plentiful and show a greater variety of hands. The Roman Uncial comes immediately after the Ptolemaic period. Different from the Ptolemaic period, the Roman Uncial, the letters were rounder and smoother, as well as being a bit larger. Additionally, with the Roman Uncial, we find decorative serifs in a number of letters, which is a slight projection finishing off a stroke of a letter. Kenyon says that P46 is a good New Testament example of the Roman Uncial.

On P46, Comfort writes, "Kenyon dated this codex to the first half of the third century. Kenyon's dating was largely influenced by the handwriting of the stichometrical notes at the end of several of the epistles, which he dated to the early part of the third century. Ulrich Wilcken, who was director of the Vienna library and founder of Archiv für Papyrusforschung, thought it belonged to the second century and said it could be dated safely to around A.D. 200. Wilcken suggested this date on the basis of seeing only one leaf. Hans Gerstinger also thought it belonged to the second century." Many "similarities are seen in the following manuscripts:

P. Oxy. 8 (assigned late first or early second century)—very similar morphologically

P. Oxy. 841 (the second hand, which cannot be dated later than a.d. 125–150 [see plate and discussion in C. H. Roberts, Greek Literary Hands, no. 14])—the handwriting is similar to that found in P46

P. Oxy. 1622 (dated with confidence to pre-a.d. 148, probably during the reign of Hadrian [117–138], because of the documentary text on the verso)—this early-dated specimen shares many similar features with P46

P. Oxy. 2337 (assigned to the late first century)—very similar but probably earlier than P46

P. Oxy. 3721 (assigned to the second half of the second century, but Kim would date it earlier)—the most comparable of all the manuscripts I have personally seen

P. Rylands III 550 (assigned to the second century)—a remarkable likeness to P46

P. Berol. 9810 (early second century)—quite similar (see plate and discussion in Schubart, Palaeographie, Handbuch der Altertumswissenschaft, 1.4.1 [Munich: C. H. Beck, 1925], 29b.)

Another reasonable way to date P46 (P. Chester Beatty II) is to compare it with the other manuscripts with which it was discovered. The earliest manuscript in this collection is unquestionably P. Chester Beatty VI (Numbers–Deuteronomy). This manuscript, displaying a good example of a Roman type of hand, is very comparable to the great Hyperides manuscript,

THE P52 PROJECT

P. London 132 (early second century A.D.); the Herodas manuscript, P. Egerton 1 (ca. A.D. 100); and P. Oxy. 270 (a documentary text dated A.D. 94). Thus, Beatty VI should be dated around A.D. 125. P46 (P. Chester Beatty II) is probably not as early as Beatty VI; indeed, it seemed to Kenyon that P46 had "lost a little of the simplicity of the best of the Roman hands." In the final analysis, P46 belongs to the second century and probably belongs to the middle part of that century, when we consider its undeniable comparability with P. Oxy. 1622 (ca. A.D. 117–138), P. Oxy. 3721 (second half of second century), P. Rylands III 550 (second century), P. Berol 9810 (early second century), and P. Oxy. 841 (second hand; 125–150).

Image Excursion

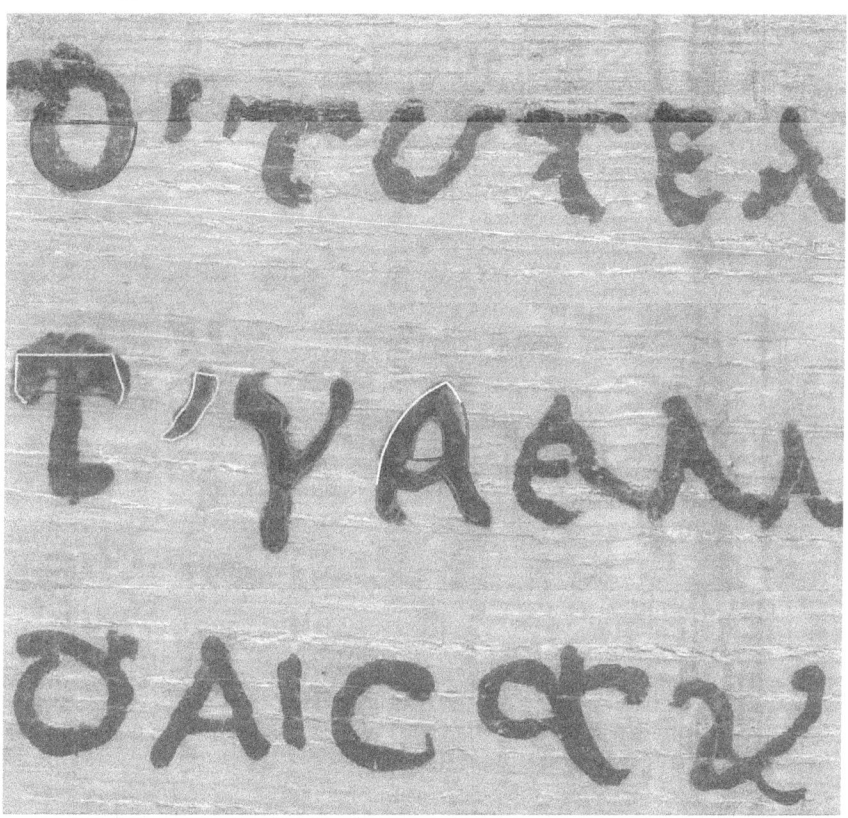

Line overlay showing similarity of letterforms

*Figure 3.1 Comparative Overlay of Papyrus P52 and P. Oxy. 841 highlighting the Greek letters **mu (μ)**, **tau (τ)**, and **upsilon (υ)**. The transparent overlay illustrates morphological congruence in stroke structure and letterform across both manuscripts, reinforcing the early second-century dating of P52*

This image presents a semi-transparent overlay comparing select Greek letters from **Papyrus P52 (Rylands Greek P 457)** and **P. Oxy. 841**, both dated to the early to mid-second century C.E. The comparative visualization demonstrates the stylistic consistency of letterforms—particularly **mu, tau, and upsilon**—between these two manuscripts. Such paleographic agreement supports the position that P52 was copied within the same scribal tradition and timeframe as other securely dated second-century texts.

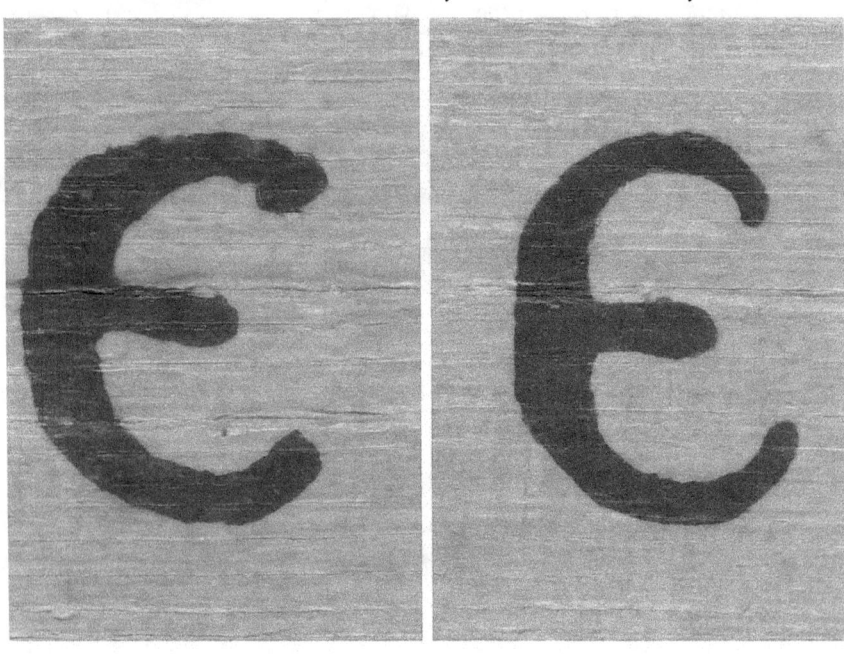

P52   P. Oxy. 1622

Figure 3.2: Side-by-Side Comparison of Greek Epsilon (*e*) in P52 and P. Oxy. 1622

Figure 3.2 Side-by-Side Comparison of Greek Epsilon (ε) in P52 and P. Oxy. 1622

Epsilon (ε) is one of the **most diagnostic letters** used by paleographers in dating early manuscripts. P. Oxy. 1622 is securely dated **before 148 C.E.**, making it an excellent comparative anchor. In P52, the epsilon often displays a **high cross-stroke** and **rounded form**, similar to second-century stylistic norms seen in P. Oxy. 1622. This comparison **visually reinforces Chapter 2–3 textual argument** that P52 shares formal features with dated documents, helping readers "see" what scholars like Roberts, Bell, and Schubart saw.

Comfort continues,

Thus, it is my opinion that P46 belongs to an era after A.D. 81–96 (the era posited by Kim)—perhaps the middle of the second century. Dating P46 to this era allows time for the formation of the Pauline corpus to have occurred and for an archetypal collection to have been produced and to circulate in Egypt. Zuntz figured that an archetypal Pauline corpus was formed by A.D. 100 in Alexandria. Thus, an Alexandrian copy such as P46 could have been produced shortly thereafter and been used by Egyptian Christians in Alexandria and other nearby towns such as Aphroditopolis (see the discussion of the provenance of the related manuscript P45)."

The Biblical Uncial or Biblical Majuscule

Image Papyrus 67 P67, which is part of P4 and P64. Date: c. 150-175 C.E.

The name does not mean that it only applies to biblical manuscripts, as it does not. The name was coined by Grenfell and Hunt, which came about from Codex Vaticanus (300-330 C.E.), Sinaiticus (330-360 C.E.), and Alexandrinus (400-440 C.E.) Majuscule is a reference to the large uncial letters. Each letter is a separate stroke from another, no letter touching. There is a simplicity and regularity to these letters. The letters' characteristics are regular, uniform, consistent, evenly shaped, and aligned. When looking at the biblical uncial of the late 3rd and early 4th centuries, the writing epsilon and the sigma ended in a very thin line that would then thicken into a dot at the end. The horizontal stroke in the epsilon, eta, and theta were thin and either in the middle or high in the letter. The base of the delta and the cross stroke of the pi were also thin, and general never protruded beyond the letter. You will also notice that the scribe made an intentional effort to have a thick vertical stroke and thin horizontal strokes and sloping strokes. Those letters that are meant to be rounded are truly circular. With the biblical uncial, the scribe made every effort to keep his text within an imagined upper and lower line, that is, a bilinear form.

ΔΕΟΠΕΤΡΟΣΑΥΤΩΕΙΠ

Decorated Rounded Uncial

Image Lower part of col. 18 (according to E. Tov) of the Greek Minor Prophets Scroll from Nahal Hever (8HevXII gr). The arrow points at the divine name in paleo-Hebrew script

On the Decorated Rounded Uncial, Comfort writes, "Another style of handwriting was prominent during the early period of the church; it is called the Decorated Rounded Uncial. In this style, every vertical stroke finishes with a serif or decorated roundel. Schubart (naming this style Zierstil) thought this style existed from the last century of the Ptolemaic period (first century BC) to the end of the first century AD. Other scholars, such as Turner, see it as extending to the end of the second century (and perhaps even into the early third). He said, "The classification 'Formal round' is attained by far fewer hands. They are almost instantly recognizable, if only from the generous size of their letters." He sees this as a single feature of several styles that existed from the second century BC to the second century AD. Concurring with Turner, Parsons writes: "Turner rightly insists that Schubart's 'decorated style'… is not really a style but a single feature of several styles spread over a period of four centuries from ii BC." Whether it is a single style or a single feature of several styles, manuscripts with the Decorated Rounded type of handwriting are conspicuous."

Severe Style

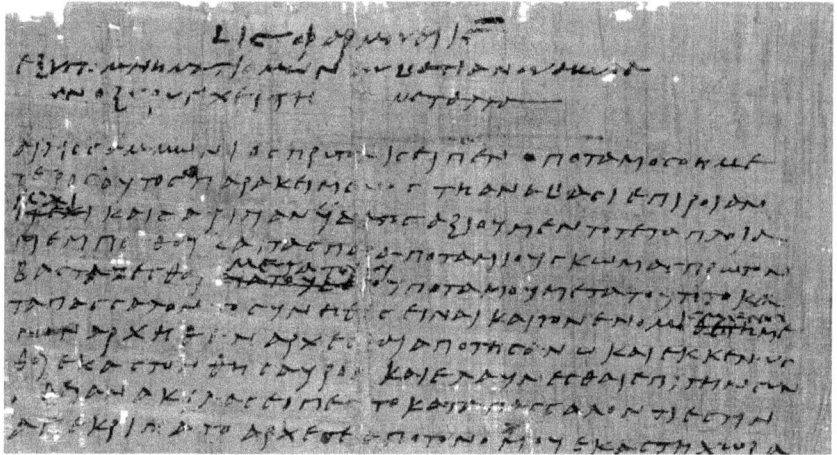

Image P. Oxyrhynchus 2341 (April 11, 208 C.E.) Documentary: Judicial Records (Proceedings)

On the Severe Style, Comfort writes, "For the most part, formal Greek handwriting remained upright during the Ptolemaic and Roman periods. In due course, however, writers began to slant their letters to the right. When handwriting is upright, the angles will be right angles and the curves will be more rounded. When handwriting slopes, the angularity of the broad letters will be emphasized, and the curves look like ellipses. This kind of hand also displays a mixture of narrow letters and broad letters. Turner, therefore, calls it Formal Mixed, while Schubart names it Strenge Stil (Severe style). Turner was of the opinion that there was no effort in documents to make a contrast between broad and narrow letters before the age of Hadrian (117–138). (See Turner's discussion in GMAW, pp. 26–27.) This is countered by G. Cavallo in his work, Libri scritture scribi a Ercolano, who makes it quite clear that documents displaying wide and narrow letters appeared in Herculaneum prior to the second century." This style can be found in the second to the early fourth centuries C.E.

Treasure from a Garbage Dump

In 1920 the John Rylands Library of Manchester, England, attained a heap of papyruses recently discovered in an ancient Egyptian garbage dump. As he sorted out the pieces of unpublished papyri, which encompassed letters, receipts, and census documents, scholar Colin H. Roberts caught sight of a fragment inscribed with text he recognized—a few verses from John chapter 18. Based on the style of the script, Roberts dated this scrap as the earliest Christian Greek text identified up to that time, even to date. It is the early date of P52 that holds its greatest value. Bible critics had argued that the Gospel of John was not penned until the second century, which would mean that the apostle John was not its author. The finding of P52 establishes that John had to be written before the close of the first century C.E., to be copied in Fayum or Oxyrhynchus, Egypt, about 110-150 C.E.

This fragment came to be known as the John Rylands Papyrus 457, designated as P52 because it was penned on papyrus. It was written in Greek uncials and has been dated to about 100-150 C.E., within just a few decades of the original writing of the Gospel of John! Significantly, even though the text only comprises a few verses, the text agrees almost precisely with the Alexandrian family of manuscripts. Its contents include John 18:31-33, 37-38.

CHAPTER 3 Colin H. Roberts and P52

ROBERTS: CBE (8 June 1909 – 1990) was a classical scholar and publisher. He was Secretary to the Delegates of Oxford University Press between 1954 and 1974. In 1934 he was elected a Junior Research Fellow at St John's, and remained a fellow there until 1976. Under the influence of his tutors, Roberts became interested in papyrology and in the history of the book in ancient times. He participated in the excavations at Karanis organized by the University of Michigan and published some Biblical papyri in the collections of the John Rylands Library. During World War II, he worked in intelligence in London and Bletchley Park. In 1948 he was elected Reader in Documentary Papyrology at Oxford. In 1954 he succeeded A. L. P. Norrington as Secretary to the Delegates of Oxford University Press, holding the post until 1974. During his tenure he oversaw the publication of the New English Bible. He was appointed CBE in 1973.

Below, we give you almost everything in C. H. Roberts' 1935 An Unpublished Fragment of the Fourth Gospel in the John Rylands Library. Manchester University Press. It is far more than you need to establish how he came to the date of 100-150 C.E. for P52.

Colin H. Roberts An Unpublished Fragment of the Fourth Gospel

THE discovery of the famous Chester Beatty biblical papyri now in course of publication, followed close by that of the Unknown Gospel (P. Egerton 2) in the British Museum, has added so much to our knowledge of the history of the text and of the way in which it was produced (with all that this involves for the study of early Christianity in general) and at the same time has opened up so wide a field for speculation that a new piece of evidence, however small, is of quite peculiar interest. This must be the excuse for the separate publication here of a small fragment whose text is given below, one of the as yet unpublished papyri in the possession of the John Rylands Library, which contains on the recto part of verses 31-33 on the verso part of verses 37-38 of ch. xvii of St. John's Gospel. (The fact that it is part of a codex, not of a roll, need now cause no surprise; thanks to recent discoveries we are coming to regard the codex as the normal vehicle for Christian literature even in the second century.) Its importance may be stated very briefly: if the argument of the present article is correct, it is the earliest known fragment of any part of the New Testament and probably the earliest witness to the existence of the Gospel according to St. John. As this claim rests solely upon considerations of palaeography, it is as well to turn our attention to this before embarking on the discussion of other problems, none the less interesting if incapable of a final solution, which such a text suggests.

Any exact dating of book hands is, of course, out of the question; all we can do is to compare the script as a whole and the forms of particular letters with those found in other texts and particularly in dated documents. A glance at the accompanying photograph shows the distinct character of our text; the scribe writes in a heavy, rounded and rather elaborate hand, often uses several strokes to form a single letter (cf. the eta and particularly the sigma in Recto, 1. 3) with a rather clumsy effect and is fond of adding a small flourish or hook to the end of his strokes (cf. the omega, the iota and the upsilon); among particular letters the epsilon with its cross stroke a little above the centre, the delta, the upsilon and the mu may be noted. Some of these features can be paralleled from dated documents; but before citing any of these it will be convenient to mention two literary texts to which it bears a striking resemblance. The first of these is no. 19 (c) in Schubart's Papyri Graecae Berolinenses, part of a roll containing Iliad, Bk. IX, assigned to the end of the first or beginning of the second century in the original publication, but which Schubart now prefers to date to the closing decades of the first century; in spite of some differences (notably the alpha which is of an earlier type) the Berlin text presents the closest parallel to our text that I have been able to find a view which I was glad to find shared by so great an authority as Sir Frederic Kenyon. The second text and this resemblance, by no means the only one between the two manuscripts, is suggestive is P. Egerton 2, assigned by the editors to the middle of the second century, a judgment which, as they remark, errs, if at all, on the side of caution. Although P. Egerton 2 is written in a lighter and less laboured hand, the family resemblance between the two is unmistakable; the forms of the upsilon, the mu and the delta in the two texts are akin and most of the characteristics of our hand are to be found, though in a less accentuated form, in P. Egerton 2. To turn to dated documents; here the most important parallels are P. Fayum no (A.D. 94), which shows, as does our text, the simultaneous use of two forms of alpha, and, less close, New Palaographical Society II, 98 (P. Lond. 2078, a private letter written in the reign of Domitian), while of interest for forms of particular letters are P. Oslo 22, a petition dated in A.D. 127 (n.b. the eta, the mu and the iota) and Schubart, Griechische Palaographie, Abb. 34 (p. 59), a document written before the death of Trajan in A.D. 117. If only to exemplify the need of caution, it should be mentioned that Sir Frederic Kenyon, while of the opinion that the affinities of the text are early rather than late and that one can hardly go wrong in dating it in the first half of the second century, points out that some similarities are to be found in P. Flor. i, a cursive document of A.D. 153. In this text the upsilon, the omega and sometimes the alpha are similar to those in our text, but other letters are radically different and its general style is not very close to that of P. Ryl. Gk. 457. On the whole we may accept with some confidence the first half of the second century as the period in which P. Ryl. Gk. 457 was most probably written a judgment I should be much more loth to pronounce were it not supported by Sir Frederic Kenyon, Dr. W. Schubart and Dr. H. I. Bell who have seen photographs of the text and whose experience and authority in these matters are unrivalled.

A few other palaeographical niceties deserve mention. In employing the diaeresis both properly (as in R. 1. 2) and improperly (e.g. in in V. 1. 2) and in omission of the iota adscript our papyrus is in agreement with P. Egerton 2; that both these practices are not inconsistent with a date in the first half of the second century has been clearly shewn by the editors of that text and needs no discussion here. The writer of P. Ryl. Gk. 457 (as far as one can judge from the scanty evidence) used neither stops nor breathings; his orthography, apart from a couple of itacisms, is good and his writing, if not that of a practised scribe, is painstaking and regular. In this respect the verdict of the editors of P. Egerton 2 upon the writer of that text is applicable to ours: P. Ryl. Gk. 457 also has a somewhat "informal air" about it and with no claims to fine writing is yet a careful piece of work. But there is one point on which P. Ryl. Gk. 457 in all probability differs from P. Egerton 2, and as it may be of importance for the date, it is as well, to consider it now: that is, the method of writing the nomina sacra. Throughout P. Egerton 2 certain nomina sacra are invariably contracted in accordance with what is almost universal practice and the contraction marked by a horizontal line drawn over the top of the letters. Unfortunately, none of the nomina sacra which are abbreviated either in P. Egerton 2 or in the Chester Beatty codex of Gospels and Acts occur in the surviving text of our fragment, but in R. 1. 5 where Ἰησοῦν must be supplied it is probable that this which, if any of the nomina sacra (to judge from later practice), would be contracted, was left unabbreviated; if it was uncontracted, the line would contain 32 letters, or 33 if Πειλᾶτος is read for Πιλᾶτος; if contracted to, there would be only 28 letters, whereas the average number of letters per line for the four lines where no possible nomina sacra are to be supplied, is 33, () found in the Chester Beatty papyri of the early third century is also a possibility, but the editors of P. Egerton 2 suggest that ΙΗ may be the earlier form). In Recto 1. 2 Ἰησοῦ could be contracted and there would remain either 31 or 32 letters to the line according to the form of the contraction; but the probability is that the nomina (or at least Ἰησοῦς) were uncontracted in this text. Not much stress can be laid on this argument, especially as we must reckon with the possibility of varieties of spelling or text in the missing passages ; but still it remains a slight support for the early date to which the manuscript has been assigned on palaeographical grounds. For while it is no doubt true that the presence of the abbreviated nomina sacra in a manuscript is no evidence against a second century date (as in the case of P. Egerton 2), especially as the practice was probably Jewish in origin and is found in early papyri of the Septuagint such as P. Baden 56 and the Chester Beatty codex of Numbers and Deuteronomy, both of the second century, yet this would make it more difficult to assign a late date to a manuscript in which Ἰησοῦς at least for θεὸς and Κυριος the text supplies no evidence remains uncontracted, suggesting as it does that either the Christian sacred books were not yet on a par with the Septuagint or that a canon was not yet established.

Another question of bibliographical interest remains to which an answer must be attempted what was the size of the original codex and how much did it contain? Part of seven lines both on recto and verso are preserved together with part of the inner margin so that it is possible to calculate not only the amount of text contained in a single page, but also the length of the line and the size of the page. The average number of letters to the line is 33 on -the recto and 29/30 on the verso, (This disparity is explained, as Mr. T. G. Skeat has pointed out to me, by the fact that whereas on the verso the scribe was writing toward the inner margin and would be limited by the fold of the leaf, i.e. if he wrote too close the initial letters of the right-hand columns of the outer leaves would be obscured, on the recto he was writing towards the outer margin and so could allow himself more latitude.) Eleven lines would be required to fill the gap between recto and verso: this gives us a page of eighteen lines and allowing for a lower margin of the same height as the upper, the codex would have been a little over 21 cm. high while its breadth assuming that the margin was uniform would be c. 20 cm. Making allowance for the fact that the lines on the verso were slightly shorter than those on the recto, we can estimate that the entire Gospel of St. John would occupy 130 pages or, with title-page, probably 66 leaves. What is slightly surprising is the size of the codex relative to the quantity of text it contained. A comparison with the Chester Beatty codex of Gospels and Acts is interesting: this, measuring 10 x 8 inches (as compared with the 8-25 x 8 inches of P. Ryl. Gk. 457) with 39 lines to the page and nearly 50 letters to the line, contained all five books within 220 pages or no leaves. A codex written on the scale of P. Ryl. Gk. 457, in order to contain the four Gospels alone, would have to consist of approximately 288 leaves. Although it would be unsafe to be dogmatic, it is highly unlikely that, at this early date, a papyrus codex of such a size would have been manufactured. (The largest of the Chester Beatty codices, from the figures given by the editor, seems to have been that of Isaiah which when complete would have consisted of a single quire of 112 leaves.) It is far more probable that the codex to which this fragment belonged contained nothing but the one Gospel; we may then compare it with P. Oxy. 208 +1781, a third-century papyrus codex of St. John's Gospel, 2f-letters to the line would have consisted when complete of 50 leaves. This is not in itself surprising, especially when we remember that this Gospel was not immune from attack as late as the end of the second century and in some circles at least was not regarded as being of equal authority with the Synoptic Gospels. Kenyon has argued from the existence of the second century codex of Numbers and Deuteronomy that we should be prepared to admit that the codex may have been used for the books of the New Testament in the second century (a suggestion amply confirmed by P. Egerton 2 and the present text), and also that the Christians of that period may have been accustomed to see the four Gospels in a single book; while this discovery by no means invalidates this second suggestion, yet we may do well to reflect that in circles where the Gospels still circulated in separate codices, i.e. where the stage of including the four in a single book and consequently of regarding them as an authoritative unity had not been reached, it would be considerably easier to explain the existence of such an apparently orthodox and respectable "fifth gospel" as that represented by P. Egerton 2. Why the early Christian communities should have preferred to have their sacred books written in the codex form rather than in the common roll form remains as obscure as ever; it may be re- marked in passing that the papyrus codex was cheaper than the roll in that both sides of the papyrus could be utilised with the minimum of inconvenience to the reader, although in this case, to judge from the spacing and the size of the hand, it is unlikely that the format was affected by considerations of economy.

Unfortunately, the provenance of the papyrus cannot be exactly determined. It was one of a large number purchased for the Library by the late B. P. Grenfell in 1920; the group to which it belongs consists of some literary texts and documents of the Ptolemaic and Roman periods, all of which are stated to have come either from the Fayum or from Oxyrhynchus. Considering the enormous number of papyri found in both of these districts, this information is not of very much value, The editors of P. Egerton 2 note that Oxyrhynchus is "the most natural place of origin for the Gospel fragments": it would be most interesting if it could be proved that these two texts, similar in several respects, were of the same provenance, but the evidence at our disposal is too slight to admit of any such proof, and we must be content with the hypothesis that they may both have originated from the same early Christian community in Middle Egypt.

Clearly no deductions can be drawn from so small a fragment as to the affinities or quality of the text itself; the only new contribution it has to make to textual criticism is the probable omission of the second εις τουτο in v. 38 (v. note). But it may well have some bearing on the wider problem as to the date of the Gospel -according to St. John. Not only is it the earliest text of the Gospel; it is also most probably the earliest substantial evidence for the existence of the Gospel. It is clear from Justin Martyr that the Gospel was known in Rome soon after the middle of the century, and it is possible that Papias, whose writings are placed between 135 and 165, alludes to it though he does not mention it by name;" on the basis of the present discovery we may assume that it was circulating in Middle Egypt in the first half of the second century. This would imply a slightly earlier date for composition, especially if with some critics we hold that the Gospel was first intended for a select circle at Ephesus; from Ephesus to Middle Egypt is a far cry, and in the case of the Unknown Gospel the editors (The New Gospel Fragments, p. 17) allow for a time-lag of about thirty years between the date of composition and that of the MS. But all we can safely say is that this fragment tends to support those critics who favour an early date (late first to early second century) for the composition of the Gospel rather than those who would still regard it a work of the middle decades of the second century. 18 But to trespass on these fields is to go beyond the limits proper to the present writer: de hac re viderint sapientiores.

In our fragment the recto the side on which the fibres of the papyrus run parallel to the writing precedes the verso; if, as was the usual practice, 19 the sheets before folding were laid with the recto side uppermost, the succession of pages on the sheet would have been verso, recto, recto, verso and our fragment would belong to the second leaf of the bifolium; but there is nothing to determine the arrangement of the codex. There are no traces of numeration.

The text is given below exactly as it appears in the papyrus except that the words have been divided. A dot below a letter denotes that it is either badly mutilated or that very small traces of it remain ; square brackets [ ] indicate lacunae (which have been filled up from the text of Westcott and Hort, double-Square brackets [[ ]] 1 an erasure by the scribe, angular brackets < > an addition to the text of the MS., round brackets ( )-in this publication only a letter whose presence or absence in the text is uncertain.

Recto (c. XVIII, vv. 31-33)

οι ϊουδαι[οι] ημε[ιν ουκ εξεστιν αποκτειναι]
ουδενα ϊνα ο λο̣[γος του ιησου πληρωθη ον ει]
πεν σημαινω[ν ποιω θανατω ημελλεν απο-]
θνησκειν ισ[ηλθεν ουν παλιν εις το πραιτω-]
ριον ο π[(ε)ιλατος και εφωνησεν τον Ἰησουν]
και ειπ[εν αυτω συ ει ο βασιλευς των ιου-]
[δ]αιω[ν απεκριθη ιησους κτλ.

Verso (c. XVIII, vv. 37-38)

[βασι-]
[λευς ειμι εγω εις το]υτο γ[ε]γεννημαι
[και ‹εις τουτο› εληλυθα εις τον κο]σμον ϊνα μαρτυ-
[ρησω τη αληθεια πας ο ων]εκ της αληθε̣[ι-]
[ας ακουει μου της φωνης] λεγει αυτω
[ο π(ε)ιλατος τι εστιν αληθεια κ]αι τουτο̣
[ειπων παλιν εξηλθεν προς] τους ιο̣[υ-]
[δαιους και λεγει αυτοις εγω ουδ]εμι[αν]

Recto I 1. ὑμῖν: 4 1. Εἰσῆλθεν

Recto 1-2. It is clear that the scribe did not adopt the common practice, found among other texts in P. Egerton 2, of indicating either the beginning or the end of a speech by leaving a small blank space; so we cannot reckon with this in calculating the length of the lines or the size of the page. In 1. i a diaeresis should perhaps be placed over the final iota of Ἰουδαῖοι; the traces are too faint to decide whether this is the case or whether the scribe, as in v. 1. 6 made an iota reaching above the level of the line.

4-5. In placing πάλιν before εἰς τὸ πραιτώριον, our papyrus agrees with the Vaticanus, the Codex Ephraemi and the restored text of the Codex

Bezae, some other MSS. and the Armenian and one of the Syrian versions (followed by the text of Westcott and Hort) ; the reverse order is supported among MSS. by the Sinaiticus and the Alexandrinus, by the Gothic version and another Syriac version and is maintained by Tischendorf.

Verso 2. If the full text is supplied in this line, we are left with 38 letters to the line in place of the average 29/30; consequently it is fairly certain that our text represents a shorter version. Most probably we should reckon with the omission of the repeated εἰς τοῦτο, perhaps a slip, but more probably a genuine variant, although unsupported by any other MS.

3. The letter after αληθ seems to have been corrected or erased: possibly we should read αληθ[[θ]], but probably the scribe's pen slipped while he was making the epsilon.

A Review and Observation of Colin H. Roberts

Being that P52, by its very nature, is a literary text, there is no date on the text or any indicator within the text itself, enabling us to know explicitly when it was dated. Roberts writes, "If the argument of the present article is correct," P52 "is the earliest known fragment of any part of the New Testament and probably the earliest witness to the existence of the Gospel according to St. John. As this claim rests solely upon considerations of palaeography." (pp. 12-13). He goes on to say, "Any exact dating of book hands is, of course, out of the question; all we can do is to compare the script as a whole and the forms of particular letters with those found in other texts and particularly in dated documents." (p. 13). "Some of these features [of P52] can be paralleled from dated documents." (p. 13). Thus, we will see that from Roberts' forward; it has been as he stated, (1) the evidence points to P52 being the earliest NT document (as of 1935), (2) it is impossible to establish an exact date, the date range (100-150 C.E.) will be (3) based entirely on paleography, (4) that is, a comparison of other literary texts and dated texts, documentary hands (contracts, petitions, letters).

Papyrologists Brent Nongbri, who has sought a redating of P52 to 100-225 C.E., writes, "Paleography is not the most effective method for dating texts, particularly those written in a literary hand. Roberts himself noted this point in his edition of P52." (p. 46). "Using other biblical papyri often regarded as early (P46, P66, P90, etc.) to date P52 (or vice versa) is also an unhelpful exercise." - Brent Nongbri (2005) The Use and Abuse of P52: Papyrological Pitfalls in the Dating of the Fourth Gospel. Harvard Theological Review 98:1, 23-48 (Bold mine)

Nongbri also wrote, "Even though some literary papyri have come to light that bear a resemblance to P52 (most notably P.Oxy. 64.4404 [now $\mathfrak{P}$104], a small fragment of Matthew's gospel dated by its editor to the second half of the second century), they are of no help in the present project since they are themselves paleographically dated. Although Turner recommends comparing literary hands with literary hands, such a process can become very circular without the inclusion of some firmly dated (usually documentary) manuscripts to act as a control. Thus, using other biblical papyri often regarded as early (P46, P66, P90, etc.) to date P52 (or vice versa) is also an unhelpful exercise. For this reason, Schmidt's arguments in 'Zwei Anmerkungen' (pp. 11-12) are not very strong." (p 46). (Bold mine)

Everyone knows that paleographic dating is conditional and difficult. No one has argued that it is the "most effective method." Every book on textual criticism and paleography makes this patently clear. There is not one papyrologist, paleographer, or textual scholar who is unaware of the immense difficulty of finding suitable comparative manuscripts. Of course, there is going to be a measure of subjectivity when one is evaluating the similarities. Yes, there are going to be difficulties in assigning dates to various paleographical features when we are dealing with literary documents, which is what Bible manuscripts are. Yes, it would be great to have corroborating documentary dated manuscripts if at all possible, which we do. And, yes, we would love to have internal evidence in P52 or any other NT manuscript for that matter (e.g., an Emperor's name or some other known official) to enable us to set an absolute exact date. As we find with P4/64/67, some kind of archaeological evidence would be welcomed. P4/64/67 cannot be dated later than 200 C.E. because "it was placed in strips (perhaps as binding) for a third-century codex of Philo. Some length of time must be allowed for a well-written codex to have been used to such an extent that it was torn up and used as binding." Another example is given by Comfort, "The Gospel harmony manuscript 0212 cannot be dated later than AD 256 and is likely to be dated ca. 230 because the manuscript was discovered in the filling of an embankment erected in AD 256. A Christian house (in existence from 222 to 235) nearby the site of discovery was destroyed when the embankment was built." The sad situation is that almost all NT manuscripts cannot be dated by using archaeological evidence.

Yes, if we all lived in a perfect world, we would have dates on every manuscript, but it is what it is, and while something is "not the most effective" to some, it might be effective to others. It is a far cry from "not the most effective" to being ineffectual. When you have literary manuscripts that are used to date a literary manuscript and then someone comes along with documentary MSS: petitions, a judgment, an invitation, and a receipt to try and redate a longtime established date, this should cause a pause for concern. Moreover, P52 does have documentary support as well. Sometimes, language is used to convey things beyond the reality of what they are... "not the most effective," "an unhelpful exercise," and "not very strong" (pessimistic and hopeless) becomes a subtle message that is being conveyed beyond the reality of what is because what is difficult (not most effect/ an unhelpful exercise) is starting to become impossible in the minds of some who are supporting this new trend of redating the early papyri because it has become popular to do so. They are adding their voices to a growing movement of redating the early papyri because the movement has appeared to be making ground as it becomes successful.

What is it about literary documents that enable the paleographer to section out different hands to different periods: Ptolemaic period, Roman period, Byzantine period? If there were no literary documents in existence in the world hypothetically speaking, why would it be difficult to create definitive periods for the handwriting of the documentary documents? Again, Roberts openly states, "As this claim [earliest NT document at the time) rests solely upon considerations of palaeography..." (p. 13). "Some of these features [of P52] can be paralleled from dated documents." (p 13).

Roberts gave us two undated literary papyri as the closest comparators to P52. The first is P. 6845: Homer, Ilias 8, 433-447, which has been dated to the 1st - 2nd century C.E. (c. 75-125). On P. 6845, Roberts wrote, "Schubart now prefers to date to the closing decades of the first century; in spite of some differences (notably the alpha which is of an earlier type), the Berlin text presents the closest parallel to our text that I have been able to find a view which I was glad to find shared by so great an authority as Sir Frederic Kenyon." Roberts also used P. Egerton 2, which was dated to 150 C.E. at that time. On P. Egerton 2, he writes, "Although P. Egerton 2 is written in a lighter and less laboured hand, the family resemblance between the two is unmistakable; the forms of the upsilon, the mu and the delta in the two texts are akin and most of the characteristics of our hand are to be found, though in a less accentuated form, in P. Egerton 2." It was the comparison of Berlin Iliad P. Berol 6845 with P52 that made the 100-150 C.E. date credible.

There was a significant papyrological study by Wilhelm Schubart, which evidenced the close similarity of the hand of Berlin Iliad P. Berol 6845 to that of P. Fayum 110, which was a personal letter written by a professional scribe, in a literary hand. On this, Roberts writes, "To turn to dated documents; here the most important parallels are P. Fayum no 110 (A.D. 94), which shows, as does our text, the simultaneous use of two forms of alpha, and, less close, New Palaeographical Society II, 98 (P.Lond. 2078, a private letter written in the reign of Domitian), while of interest for forms of particular letters are P.

THE P52 PROJECT

Oslo 22, a petition dated in A.D. 127 (n.b. the eta, the mu and the iota) and Schubart, Griechische Palaographie, Abb. 34 (p. 59), a document written before the death of Trajan in A.D. 117."

Skeat and Bell had also relied on P. Fayum 110 when they dated P. Egerton 2 to around 150 C.E. They had also used a letter in a documentary hand B.G.U. 1.22 (Abb 34), which is dated to about 110-117 C.E., around the time of Trajan, as well as P.Lond. 1.130, a horoscope, letter, teacher (astrology) to students, which was dated to the late first or early second century. The Berlin Iliad P. Berol 6845 has been edited once more based on more recent studies, which have conformed the dating of about 100 C.E. by Schubart, as well as reaffirming the close correlation to the dated literary hand of P.Fayum 110. Moreover, it continues as a major example of a specifically distinctive form of the late first century to the early second century C.E. book hand handwriting style. Some 20 years after 1935, Roberts reaffirmed the close similarity of P. Fayum 110 to both P52 and P. Egerton 2.

Roberts offered yet two more documentary manuscripts (dated manuscripts) as being a close comparison to P52. P. London 2078, a private letter written in the reign of Domitian (81-96 CE), and P. Oslo 22, a petition dated to 127 C.E. Roberts noted that that P. Oslo 22 was particularly most similar in some of the more distinctive letter forms, such as the eta, mu, and iota. Roberts sent his conclusion to Sir Frederic G. Kenyon, Wilhelm Schubart, and H. I. Bell that P52 should be dated to the first half of the second century, 100-150 C.E. All three agreed with his dating of P52. Kenyon pointed out some similarities to P. Flor 1. 1, a loan contract dated 153 C.E. Two points on this comparison: (1) 153 is really not outside of Roberts dating of P52 to 100-150 C.E. (2) the similarity was not very close to P52 and P. Flor 1. 1 is a cursive document. On this Roberts rightly observed, "In this text [P. Flor 1. 1] the upsilon, the omega and sometimes the alpha are similar to those in our text, but other letters are radically different and its general style is not very close to that of P. Ryl. Gk. 457." (Page 16). We close this section with the fact that Roberts' conclusions were also supported in 1935 by an independent study by A. Deissmann, which suggested a date during the reign of Hadrian (117-138 C.E.), or even possible Trajan (98-117 C.E.). In 1936 Roberts' date of 100-150 C.E. was given additional support from Ulrich Wilcken, to which Philip W. Comfort writes, "Another two hundred Greek documentary papyri, dated AD 113–120, have come from the archive of Apollonios, a strategos of Hermopolis. A thorough study of these manuscripts prompted the papyrologist Ulrich Wilcken to date P52 to the same era, on the basis of comparable paleography."

See PHOTOGRAPHS OF THE EARLY MANUSCRIPTS at the end of this publication.

Appendix A: Early Christian Codex Culture and the Context of P52

The significance of Papyrus P52 cannot be rightly assessed apart from the codicological revolution that took place within early Christianity during the late first and early second centuries C.E. While the Greco-Roman world at large retained a strong preference for the scroll (volumen), Christian communities quickly and consistently favored the codex form. This preference was not merely incidental but reflects theological, practical, and cultural dynamics unique to early Christianity—factors that help contextualize the production of P52.

The Emergence of the Codex in Christian Circles

By the early second century, Christians began producing a significant number of their texts in codex format. Manuscript finds from Egypt such as **P. Chester Beatty I (P45)**, **P. Chester Beatty II (P46)**, and **P. Bodmer II (P66)**—all codices containing New Testament writings—date from the second century. These were not outliers. Across various Christian textual traditions, the codex became the preferred medium for transcribing Scripture. Among Greek literary texts as a whole, codices represented only about 5% of manuscript finds dated to the second century. But among Christian texts, that percentage skyrockets to over 90%, even by the mid-second century.

Why Christians Preferred the Codex

There are several reasons for this marked departure from prevailing scribal culture:

1. **Portability and Compactness**: Codices allowed more text in a smaller space. For itinerant missionaries and teachers, this was vital. Paul's letters, the Gospels, and various collections could be copied and carried with ease in codex form.

2. **Accessibility for Public Reading**: Early Christian worship involved the public reading of Scripture (cf. 1 Timothy 4:13). A codex allowed faster navigation between texts than the linear scroll format.

3. **Doctrinal Emphasis**: The very physical form of the codex may have reinforced the idea of a unified body of sacred writings—an emerging "canon." A codex could unite four Gospels or a Pauline corpus, suggesting intentional theological collection.

4. **Cultural Identity**: As Christianity increasingly distinguished itself from Judaism and Greco-Roman religious life, its distinctive codex use became a form of cultural and religious self-definition.

Codicology and the Dating of P52

P52, a fragment from a single-quire codex, fits squarely within this early Christian scribal trend. Its physical characteristics—a single column of text on each side, relatively narrow margins, and a clean uncial hand—are consistent with second-century Christian book production. While its textual contents (from the Gospel of John) and paleographic features have rightly drawn scholarly attention, the codicological aspect reinforces its Christian origin and fits chronologically within the period when the codex was not yet dominant in the broader literary world but had already become standard among Christian scribes.

Supporting Data from Other Codices

Consider the following early Christian codices:

- **P46**: Contains much of the Pauline corpus, dated ca. 175–225 C.E. Codex form.

- **P66**: Gospel of John, dated ca. 175–200 C.E. Codex form.

- **P45**: Portions of the Gospels and Acts, dated ca. 200–250 C.E. Codex form.

- **P. Egerton 2**: An apocryphal Gospel, dated early second century. Codex form.

- **P. Oxy. 4009**: A Christian epistle fragment, dated ca. 150–200 C.E. Codex form.

Even early apocryphal and non-canonical texts followed this trend, emphasizing that the preference for the codex was not driven by canonical status but by broader Christian use.

Conclusion

The codicological form of P52—namely, that it came from a Christian codex—complements its paleographic features and helps narrow its historical context. This cultural commitment to the codex by early Christians was a deliberate choice reflecting both theological values and practical needs. It is in this codicological and ecclesiastical setting that P52 finds its most plausible historical home: among early Christian communities copying sacred texts for worship, teaching, and transmission, not long after the turn of the second century C.E.

Table A.1: Early Christian Codices (Second–Early Third Century C.E.)

Manuscript	Contents	Estimated Date	Codex Format	Notes
P52 (P. Rylands Gr. 457)	Gospel of John (18:31–33, 37–38)	110–150 C.E.	Single-quire codex	Oldest known NT fragment; supports early use of codex by Christians
P. Egerton 2	Unnamed apocryphal gospel	ca. 100–150 C.E.	Single-quire codex	Non-canonical; shows early Christian codex use beyond canonical texts
P. Oxy. 4009	Christian epistle	ca. 150–200 C.E.	Codex	Christian theological content in codex format
P46 (Chester Beatty II)	Pauline Epistles (10 of 13)	100–150 C.E.	Multiple-quire codex	Large corpus with editorial coherence; possible proto-canonical function
P66 (Bodmer II)	Gospel of John	ca. 125–150 C.E.	Single-quire codex	Nearly complete Gospel; codex form from early stage of textual transmission
P45 (Chester Beatty I)	Gospels and Acts (fragments)	ca. 175–225 C.E.	Multiple-quire codex	Combines Synoptic Gospels, John, and Acts—possible

THE P52 PROJECT

Manuscript	Contents	Estimated Date	Codex Format	Notes
				evangelion + Acts corpus
P75 (Bodmer XIV–XV)	Luke and John	ca. 175–225 C.E.	Single-quire codex	Careful textual transmission; notable for alignment with Vaticanus
P4 + P64 + P67	Matthew and Luke fragments	150–175 C.E.	Likely codex	Often associated by papyrologists; codicological data incomplete

This table reinforces your case that P52, as part of an early codex, fits naturally within the second-century Christian manuscript culture. Its form is not anomalous but consistent with the Christian movement's distinctive scribal practices during that period.

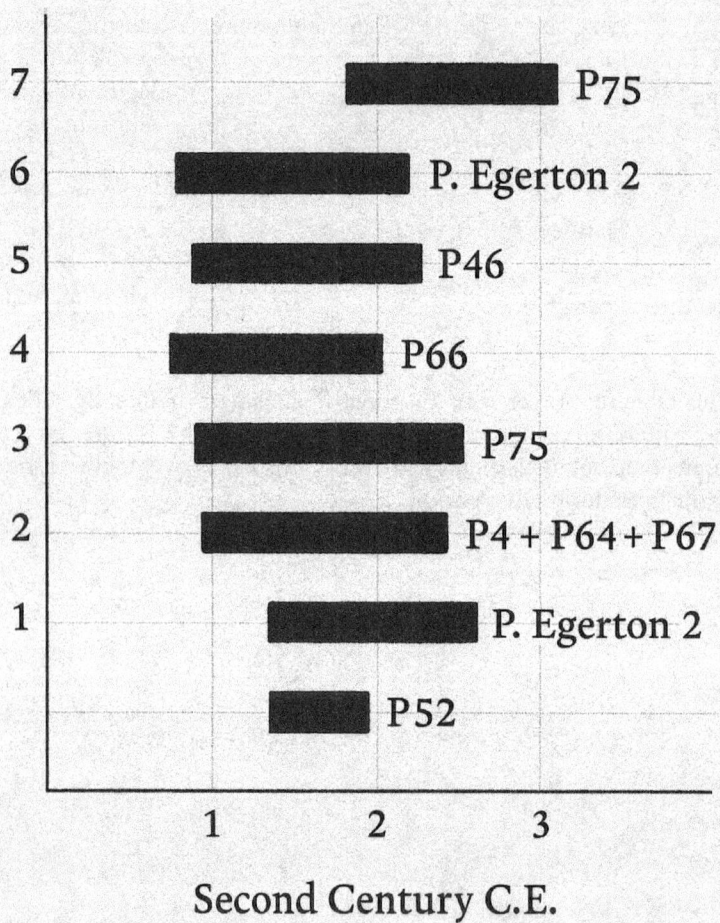

CHAPTER 4 Philip Comfort and P52

Dr. Philip Wesley Comfort (1950–) is a noted professor, author, and editor. He is a professor of Greek and New Testament at Trinity Episcopal Seminary, visiting professor at Wheaton College, and senior editor of Bible reference at Tyndale House Publishers for 25-years. Comfort completed his second doctorate under the noted textual critic Jacobus H. Petzer at the University of South Africa. Comfort has been working in the field of textual criticism, paleography, and papyrology for over thirty years and has written over fifteen books on New Testament Textual Studies, many on paleography and papyrology, the first being some thirty years ago in 1990. Comfort has examined almost all of the 5,000 Oxyrhynchus papyri collection. He has also studied all of the early New Testament papyri, 25 of them in person with the actual document. When not in person, he has used high definition images, such as The Center for the Study of New Testament Manuscripts, as well as hundreds of manuscripts from other collections. Comfort has spent most of his life researching and studying ancient papyri, deciphering what is on the papyrus, and then publishing his findings. This is the case with many past world-renowned papyrologists, such as Sir Frederic George Kenyon, Ulrich Wilcken, or E. G. Turner. The only thing Comfort has not done is work at caring for and preserving rare papyrus originals as Kenyon did at the British Museum.

Below, we will borrow extensively from two of Comfort's books so that we can have all of the evidence he has given in defense of his early dating of P52. A large section of the chapter on Philip Comfort and a few other places within THE P52 PROJECT is taken by permission from THE TEXT OF THE EARLIEST NEW TESTAMENT MANUSCRIPTS © Copyright 2019 by Philip Wesley Comfort and David P. Barrett. Published by Kregel Publications, Grand Rapids, MI. Used by permission of the publisher. All rights reserved.

Many scholars (Frederic G. Kenyon, H. I. Bell, Adolf Deissmann, and W. H. P. Hatch) have confirmed the dating of P52. Deissmann was convinced that it was written at least during the reign of Hadrian (A.D. 117–138) and perhaps even during the reign of Trajan (A.D. 98–117). Deissmann wrote an article on this, "Ein Evangelienblatt aus den Tagen Hadrians," which was translated in the British Weekly.

This dating is derived from comparing P52 to manuscripts such as P. Fayum 110 (A.D. 94), the Egerton Gospel (A.D. 130–150), P. Oslo 22 (A.D. 127), P. London 2078 (reign of Domitian, A.D. 81–96), and P. Berolinenses 6845 (ca. A.D. 100). Though each of these manuscripts bears significant resemblance to P52, P. Berolinenses 6845 is the closest parallel, in Roberts's opinion. Another manuscript shares many similarities with P52, P. Oxy. 2533. The editors of P. Oxy. 2533 said that its handwriting could be paralleled with first-century documents, but since it had the appearance of being second century, they assigned it a second-century date. Thus, both P. Oxy. 2533 and P52 can safely be dated to A.D. 100–125. However, its comparability to manuscripts of an even earlier period (especially P. Berol. 6845), pushes the date closer to A.D. 100, plus or minus a few years. This is extremely remarkable, especially if we accept the consensus dating for the composition of the Fourth Gospel: A.D. 80–85. This would mean that P52 may be only twenty years removed from the original.

P52 (P. Rylands 457), beginning of the second century (100–125).—

*C. H. Roberts, An Unpublished Fragment of the Fourth Gospel in the John Rylands Library (Manchester, 1935) This was republished with a few alterations in the Bulletin of the John Ryland's Library XX (1936) 45-55; and then again in the Catalog of the Greek and Latin Papyri in the John Ryland's Library iii (Manchester, 1938), the last publication contains critical notes and bibliography of scholarly reviews. *John 18:31-34, 37-38.

This manuscript preserves only a few verses of John's Gospel 18:31–33, 37–38). This hand, casual and rounded, clearly belongs to the early part of the second century. C. H. Roberts dated this manuscript to the first half of the second century. He noted that paleographers such as Kenyon, H. I. Bell, Deissmann, and W. H. P. Hatch confirmed this dating. Deissmann was convinced that P52 was written at least during the reign of Hadrian (117–138) and perhaps even during the reign of Trajan (98–117). The eminent papyrologist Ulrich Wilcken indicated that, as far as the paleography was concerned, P52 could be contemporary with manuscripts in the Apollonios Archives, dated AD 117–120 (the Bremer Papyri). This is quite a significant observation inasmuch as Wilcken had just completed a publication of the Bremer Papyri (which includes the Apollonios Archives) when he made this observation about P52. Therefore, he was drawing upon his keen observation of several manuscripts dated between AD 117 and 120. Though I have seen only a few manuscripts of this archive, I can see the affinity, for example, between P52 and Bremer Papyri 5, reproduced in Wilcken's work (note especially the similar formation of the alpha, delta, and epsilon). My comparative study is limited; Wilcken had far more manuscripts in making his estimation. Kurt Aland has followed the lead of the aforementioned paleographers and dated P52 "near the beginning of the second century." As such, in Aland's estimation, it is the earliest New Testament papyrus manuscript. (Of course, manuscripts such as P104, discussed later, were not available to Aland.)

THE P52 PROJECT

C. H. Roberts's dating of P52 was derived from a comparative analysis of P52 to documentary manuscripts such as P. Fayum 110 (AD 94; for photo, see GLH 11b; Montev., pl. 44), P. London 2078 (a private letter written during the reign of Domitian; AD 81–96), P. Oslo 22 (a petition dated in AD 127—note particularly the similar formation of the eta, mu, and iota), P. Berol. 6845 (late first century; for photo, see Greek Berol. 19c), P. Berol. 6854 (a document written before the death of Trajan in AD 117; for photo, see Schubart's Greek Paleography, pl. 34), and P. Egerton 2, the Egerton Gospel (dated ca. 150).

I have looked at photographs of all these manuscripts and would concur with Roberts's estimations of comparability to P52. I would especially note P. Oslo 22. Yet there is another manuscript that appears to be the very likeness of P52; it is P. Oxyrhynchus 2533. I examined the manuscript P. Oxyrhynchus 2533 at the Ashmolean Museum and was immediately impressed by its likenesss to P52. The editors of P. Oxyrhynchus 2533 said the handwriting could be parallel with first-century documents, but has the appearance of being second century (to which they dated it). I quote their comments in full:

> The text of the recto of this papyrus is a document, written in a practiced upright business hand, neat but employing cursive forms of varying sizes, all of which could be paralleled in first-century documents; the general impression, however, suggests the second century. On the verso is written a passage of New Comedy in a semi-literate hand, upright, rounded and clear; the letters are somewhat variable in size, and several (notably epsilon and kappa) show cursive forms; ligature is common. The appearance of the recto and verso texts is superficially dissimilar, but examination of the letters shows so many identical forms that it seems likely that the writer is the same.

What is not logical in this explanation is that the editors said the writing of the document "could be paralleled in first-century manuscripts" but then dated it to the second century. I would think that the document is first century and so in the New Comedy, for the literary piece would not have been written long after the documentary work. The strong similarity between this manuscript (with a firm date) and P52 helps to establish the date of P52 as being at the latest early second century (Or. A.D. 100-125).

I would also point to P. Murabbaʻat 113, a document dated to pre-AD 132. Its overall likeness to P52 is immediately apparent; one can also note the epsilon-iota combination, the alpha, and delta in both manuscripts. Both manuscripts share affinities with P. London 130 (dated early second century;

for photo, see Schubart's Greek Pal. 81) and P. Berol. 6854 (dated AD 135?; for photo, see Greek Berol. 22b).

Three other manuscripts need to be brought into the discussion, all from the Oxyrhynchus collection. The first is P. Oxyrhynchus 2367, which was discussed in detail concerning the dating of P32. The overall likeness is apparent. The second is Oxyrhynchus 4416 (Apollonius Rhodius, Agonautica), which is dated to the second century. The handwriting is extremely similar to that found in P52. The overall casual appearance is very similar and the individual formation of letters (note the similar alpha, delta, epsilon, eta, kappa, lambda, mu, nu, pi). The third manuscript is P. Oxyrhynchus 5202 (Copy of an Inscription for the Poetic Victor Arion), which is dated to the second half of the first century. The handwriting is similar to that found in P52 but earlier in overall appearance and individual letters.

Finally, I draw upon another Oxyrhynchus manuscript (P. Oxyrhynchus 5178, which is contemporaneous with P. Oxyrhynchus 5177) for dating P52 to the early second century. P. Oxyrhynchus 5177 is a letter from Diogenes, Strategus, to Heraclides, dated "27 November-December 26, 132." Concerning P. Oxyrhynchus 5177 the editor (M. Malouta) said: "The papyrus was found together with [P Oxy.] 5178, a letter from Heraclides to the Strategus Claudius Diogenes, and it is reasonable to assume that these are the same people. The letter seems to have been sent to acknowledge receipt of official correspondence from Heraclides." P. Oxyrhynchus 5178 is a letter of Heraclides to Claudius Diogenes, Strategus. Concerning its relationship to P. Oxyrhynchus 5177, the editor (also M. Malouta) said of P. Oxyrhynchus 5178: "The inventory number indicates that [P. Oxy.] 5178 was found with [P. Oxy.] 5177, a letter Diogenes, Strategus, to Heraclides, dated to 132. Though [P. Oxy.] 5178 is not exactly dated, it is probable that we are dealing with the same persons and that the two letters are contemporary." In short, P. Oxyrhynchus 5178 is easily dated to A.D. 132 or 133. It is fortunate that this dated manuscript that has handwriting that is remarkably like that of P52. One should note the same formation of the following letters: alpha, delta, epsilon, eta, iota, kappa, lambda, mu, nu, omicron, pi, rho, sigma, tau, omega (which are nearly all the letters the two manuscripts have in common; ....). Thus, we have a manuscript (P. Oxyrhynchus 5178) that greatly helps us date P52 to the early second century, at least.

In the final analysis, P52 belongs to the beginning of the second century. This dating of P52 is extremely remarkable, especially if we accept the consensus dating for the composition of the fourth Gospel: A.D. 80-85. This means that P52 is only about 25 years away from the original. I should also note that Jaros dates P52 as "A.D. 80–125."

A. Schmidt has challenged the earlier dating of P52. He has placed it near the end of the second century, close to ca. 200. This redating has appealed to some scholars, but most hold with the earlier dating and still affirm that P52 is probably the earliest New Testament manuscript. (See photos of P52 next to P. Oxy. 2533, P. Egerton 2, and P. Fayum 110 on pp. 144–45.)

A Review and Observation of Philip Comfort

The above was Taken from THE TEXT OF THE EARLIEST NEW TESTAMENT MANUSCRIPTS © Copyright 2019 by Philip Wesley Comfort and David P. Barrett. Published by Kregel Publications, Grand Rapids, MI. Used by permission of the publisher. All rights reserved.

As to Comfort and Roberts' dating of P52 and the evidence that gets us there, this author wholeheartedly agrees. However, I would disagree with the dates that Comfort has set out "for the composition of the fourth Gospel: A.D. 80-85." Most would agree that John authored his Gospel long after A.D. 70 because he makes no reference to it at all. Moreover, the date has to be before the time of Irenaeus (130-202) a student of Polycarp, who was a direct disciple of the apostle John, who quotes from the Gospel and the epistles of John in the early second century. The Gospel of John was written in Ephesus or near Ephesus, the historian Eusebius (c. 260-342 C.E.) quotes Irenaeus: "John, the disciple of the Lord, who had even rested on his breast, himself also gave forth the gospel, while he was living at Ephesus in Asia." Yes, John wrote his Gospel after his exile on the island of Patmos. (Rev. 1:9) At the beginning of his reign, the Roman Emperor Nerva (96-98 C.E.) recalled many who had been exiled. Therefore, John very much likely wrote his Gospel about A.D. 98, with John dying a peaceful death in the third year Emperor Trajan, A.D. 100 in Ephesus. P52, the John Ryland Fragment manuscript was discovered in a small town in Egypt and can be dated to about A.D.110–25. This still falls well within the dates given by C. H. Roberts in 1935, A.D.100–150. Of course, we must allow some time for the Gospel to have worked its way down into Egypt after it had been authored in A.D. 98. – Edward D. Andrews

We have been fortunate to have access to what Comfort and Barrett have written concern P52. From them, other comparator literary and documentary papyri have been suggested and should be readily accepted.

Edward D. Andrews
Comfort Addresses the P. Egerton 2 Issue

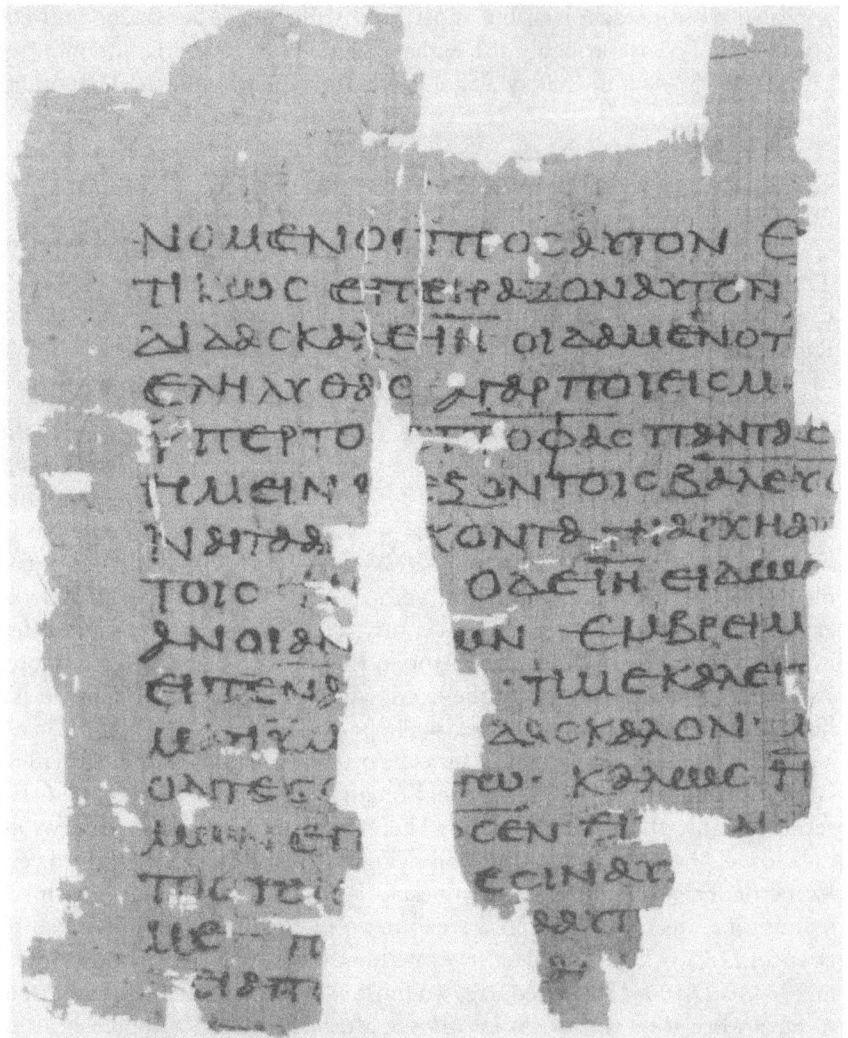

Image 20 P. Egerton 2

P. Egerton 2, Unknown Gospel. According to the editors, H. I. Bell and T. C. Skeat, this gospel was probably composed in the early part of the second century, and the copy which was discovered could be no later than 150. The paleographic dating came about by a morphological comparison with the following manuscripts: P52 (dated early second century) with which it bears unmistakable likeness; P. Berol. 6854 (a document dated in the reign of Trajan, who died in AD 117; for photo, see Schubart's Greek Pal., 34; GLH

12a); P. London 130 (a horoscope calculated from AD April 1, 81 and therefore not likely to be later than the early years of the second century; for photo see Schubart's Greek Pal., 81); and P. Oxyrhynchus 656 (Genesis, mid to late second century, see discussion above). Clearly, all these comparable manuscripts are dated within the period of late first century to second century, and most of them have solid documentary dating. Being somewhat conservative, Bell and Skeat then dated P. Egerton 2 to a date "later than the middle of the second century." In a subsequent article, Bell wrote, "This papyrus almost certainly falls within the period AD 120–170, and it is on the whole likely to date from the first rather than the second half of that period."55 (It should be noted that P. London 130 bears significant resemblance to P32; see comments there.)

A new fragment of the Egerton Gospel was published several years later as P. Köln 255. This manuscript shows the word aneneg'kon with a hook between the consonant's gamma and kappa. Because Turner argued that this was a feature prominent in the third century, the date of the Egerton Gospel is now being questioned. Indeed, the editors of P. Koln 255 cited the date as "ca. 150 (?)." Hence, the editors of this Köln fragment of the Unknown Gospel wonder if it should be ca. 200, in accordance with Turner's dating of P. Bodmer II (P66), which he dates to ca. 200 on the basis of the presence of the hook between consonants.

However, I would argue (as I did above) that Turner's dating needs to be revised not vice versa. The dating of the Egerton Gospel to the mid-second century should still stand because of its overall morphological likeness to so many manuscripts of the early to middle second century.

Turner indicates that another feature began in the early third century, namely, the use of a separating apostrophe between double consonants. Some paleographers of late seem to have adopted this observation as "fact" and thereby date manuscripts having this feature as post AD 200. Some paleographers would even redate manuscripts displaying this feature. For example, Schmidt redates P52 to ca. 200 based on the fact that its hand parallels that of the Egerton Gospel, which is now thought by some to date closer to ca. 200 based on this feature appearing in a newly published portion of the Egerton Gospel. However, I would argue that the previously assigned date of such manuscripts was given by many scholars according to their observations of several paleographic features. Thus, the presence of this particular feature (the hook or apostrophe between double consonants) determines an earlier date for its emergence, not the other way around. Thus, the Egerton Gospel, dated by many to ca. 150, should still stand, and so should the date for P52 (as early second century). Another way to come at this is to look at P66, dated by several scholars to ca. 150 (see discussion below). Turner, however, would date P66 later (early third) largely because of the presence of the hook between double consonants. What I would say is that the predominant dating of P66 (i.e., the dating assigned by most scholars) predetermines the date for this particular feature. Furthermore, there are other manuscripts dated prior to AD 200 that exhibit the apostrophe or hook between double consonants:

1. BGU iii 715.5 (AD 101)

Αγ'χωριμφις

2. P. Petaus 86 (= P. Michigan 6871) (AD 185)

Αγ'γων

3. SPP xxii 3.22 (second century)

Απυγ'χεως

4. P. Berol. 9570 + P. Rylands 60 (dated by the editors of the editio princeps to ca. 200, dated by Cavallo to ca. 50)

Φαλαγ'γας

Response and Observation

Let me just say that the biggest piece of evidence for changing the dating of P52 to 200 C.E. or later was changing the dating of P. Egerton 2 from 150 C.E. to 200 C.E. This is also what pushed the redating of P66 from 150 C.E. to 200 C.E. The problem with changing P. Egerton 2 was a hooked apostrophe between two consonants. The scholars seeking a date change misunderstood Turner's words as it relates to the hooked apostrophe. Turner said it became a practice in the third century, so the scholars redated P. Egerton 2, P52, and P66 based on a hooked apostrophe. The problem being that Turner did not say there were no cases in the second century. In fact, he cited two examples, and there are other examples cited by Comfort above. So, it was developing in the second century and became a common practice in the third century.

There is a great value in P. Egerton Papyrus 2 fragments just as it true with P52. They serve as an aid in undermining the Bible critics. These critics have long argued that John's Gospel was not written until 170 C.E. This would mean that it could not have been written by the apostle John who died seventy years earlier in 100 C.E. Since P. Egerton Papyrus 2 fragments have so many parallel expressions found in John's Gospel, it strongly indicates that whoever wrote P. Egerton Papyrus 2 fragments, he was using John's writing as a source. Then, we have P52, a fragment of John's Gospel, which has been dated to 100-150 C.E. Thus, the Gospel of John must have been written earlier than 150 C.E. for it to have been circulating down in Egypt where the Egerton Papyrus 2 fragments were written about 150 C.E. Therefore, P. Egerton Papyrus 2 fragments bolstered by the discovery in 1935 of the fragment P52 of John's Gospel (Papyrus Rylands Gk 457), which we have no reason to doubt dates to 100 – 150 C.E. to give it time to be found in Egypt, confirm the date of the writing of John's Gospel to be about 98 C.E.

Simon Gathercole, The Earliest Manuscript Title of Matthew's Gospel, Novum Testamentum 54 (2012) 209 -235

Article Abstract: A flyleaf bearing the title of Matthew's gospel, found with the Luke fragments of P4 (henceforth P4), has been neglected in studies of P4 as well as in editions of the Greek New Testament. This article publishes for the first time a photograph of the flyleaf, and seeks to provide an accurate transcription of the often misspelled title. It also discusses the various factors impinging upon the date of the fragment, such as the Philo codex in which it was found and the apostrophe in the middle of Matthew's name. A date in the late second or early third century makes best sense of the evidence, making this neglected flyleaf the earliest manuscript title of Matthew's gospel. Within this article is a lengthy discussion about the scribal habit of using an apostrophe between two consonants that was developing in the second century and became "extremely common and then persists" in the third century. This ties in with our discussion here with P. Egerton 2, the Unknown Gospel, and the redating of P52. Simon Gathercole's article is excellent and very objective, but I feel some observations need to be made. Thus, below are highlights from his article along with my responses.

ARTICLE QUOTE: Turner and Parsons have commented: "In the first decade of iii A.D. this practice suddenly becomes extremely common and then persists." (Page 227).

ARTICLE QUOTE: Oxford Handbook of Papyrology remarking that "in the third century CE, the habit arose of placing an apostrophe between doubled mutes or liquids," (Page 228).

RESPONSE: Turner said, "In the first decade of iii AD this practice [using an apostrophe between two consonants] suddenly becomes extremely common and then persists." Notice here what Turner does not say; he was not saying that this practice was not taking place in the second century at all, but rather it became "extremely common and then persists" in the third century. Then Turner goes on to give examples of using a hooked apostrophe between two consonants from the second century.

ARTICLE QUOTE: Comfort and Barrett are the two scholars (writing collaboratively) who have ventured to question the consensus view. As a result of some of these considerations outlined above, they remark: "This title sheet was probably produced around A.D. 175-200 because that is when it became stylish for scribes to insert a hooked comma (apostrophe) between double consonants—as here, between the thetas." (Page 230).

RESPONSE: Gathercole is about to question the wording from Comfort, "it became stylish." But notice turner again arguing for the third century, [became "extremely common and then persists"] and now Comfort, "became stylish." What Comfort meant was that using an apostrophe between two consonants was developing in the second century, and Turner is correct that it was in the third century that it became "extremely common and then persists." I will show this to be true after the next quote.

ARTICLE QUOTE: First, the reasons given by Comfort and Barrett for assigning a probable second century date are clearly problematic. Both the facts and the logic are faulty: it is not really true that the habit "became stylish" in the second century, and even if it had, a particular instance in a particular manuscript cannot with probability be assigned to the time when the habit first became fashionable. (Page 230-1).

RESPONSE: Then, this would be true of when it became "extremely common and then persists" too. I mean really, Comfort is only saying when it was being developed. This, if you argue that it was the third century when using an apostrophe between two consonants became "extremely common and then persists;" then, it only seems like common sense that with numerous examples from the second century, it was developing.

On this, Philip Comfort offers us a reasonable view when he writes,

> Turner indicates that another feature began in the early third century, namely, the use of a separating apostrophe between double consonants. Some paleographers of late seem to have adopted this observation as "fact" and thereby date manuscripts having this feature as post AD 200. Some paleographers would even redate manuscripts displaying this feature. For example, Schmidt redates P52 to ca. 200 based on the fact that its hand parallels that of the Egerton Gospel, which is now thought by some to date closer to ca. 200 based on this feature appearing in a newly published portion of the Egerton Gospel. However, I would argue that the previously assigned date of such manuscripts was given by many scholars according to their observations of several paleographic features. Thus, the presence of this particular feature (the hook or apostrophe between double consonants) determines

an earlier date for its emergence, not the other way around. Thus, the Egerton Gospel, dated by many to ca. 150, should still stand, and so should the date for P52 (as early second century). Another way to come at this is to look at P66, dated by several scholars to ca. 150 (see discussion below). Turner, however, would date P66 later (early third) largely because of the presence of the hook between double consonants. What I would say is that the predominant dating of P66 (i.e., the dating assigned by most scholars) predetermines the date for this particular feature. Furthermore, there are other manuscripts dated prior to AD 200 that exhibit the apostrophe or hook between double consonants:

1. BGU iii 715.5 (AD 101)
αγ'χωριμφις
2. P. Petaus 86 (= P. Michigan 6871) (AD 185)
αγ'γων
3. SPP xxii 3.22 (second century)
απυγ'χεως
4. P. Berol. 9570 + P. Rylands 60 (dated by the editors of the editio princeps to ca. 200, dated by Cavallo to ca. 50)
φαλαγ'γας

ARTICLE QUOTE: In these cases above, the apostrophe is often treated not merely as a deciding factor in favour of a third century hand all other things being equal. Rather, it is regarded by some as alone sufficient to indicate a third century date and to outweigh the other factors indicating an earlier timeframe. (Page 233).

RESPONSE: Herein lies the problem. Using an apostrophe between two consonants was developing in the second century and became "extremely common and then persists" in the third century, so we ignore the fact that is was developing and existed in the second century and start redating everything based on an apostrophe, even though prior to many scholars for many reasons dated the manuscripts earlier. I will return to this in a moment.

ARTICLE QUOTE: It is extremely difficult to evaluate the relative merits of these arguments. Perhaps one should at most conclude that the appearance of the apostrophe cannot be assigned quite the decisive significance it has had in some recent discussions. On the other side, neither should one rush to argue that an apostrophe is as likely to be second century as third. (Page 233).

RESPONSE: No one is arguing that an apostrophe is as likely, just likely, and when coupled with the other reasons for an early date, the early date should stand.

ARTICLE QUOTE: Overall, the presence of the apostrophe in the flyleaf might well play a role in nudging the date into the third century, but it should not play an absolutely decisive role. (Page 233).

RESPONSE: Agreed. But once again, you had many world-renowned scholars date some manuscripts one way and then based on an apostrophe that was developing and did exist in the second century, they redate because it became "extremely common and then persists" in the third century

ARTICLE QUOTE: The giants in the field of papyrology commonly state that the apostrophe as a consonant divider is a feature almost exclusively belonging to the third century CE and beyond. (Page 227).

RESPONSE: Usually, either side would say this is a fallacy of arguing from authority. But I can say it has to add some weight but the evidence they present is the real evidence. So, if we are going to argue "giants in the field of papyrology" then let's do it.

World-Renowned Paleographers and Textual Scholars Date P52 Early

- 100-150 C.H. Roberts
- 100-150 Sir Frederic G. Kenyon
- 100-150 W. Schubart
- 100-150 Sir Harold I. Bell
- 100-150 Adolf Deissmann
- 100-150 E. G. Turner
- 100-150 Ulrich Wilken
- 100-150 W. H. P. Hatch
- 125-175 Kurt and Barbara Aland
- 100-150: Philip W. Comfort
- 100-150 Bruce M. Metzger
- 100-150 Daniel B. Wallace
- 125-175 Pasquale Orsini
- 125-175 Willy Clarysse

The New Uncertain and Ambiguous Minded Textual Scholars Date P52

- 100-225 Brent Nongbri
- 200-300 Michael Gronewald

CHAPTER 5 Brent Nongbri and P52

Brent Nongbri did his Ph.D. in New Testament at Yale and is an Honorary Research Fellow at Macquarie University in Sydney, Australia, and the author of Before Religion: A History of a Modern Concept and numerous articles on the paleography and codicology of early Christian manuscripts.

The early date for P52 [100-150 C.E.] was favored by New Testament textual scholars since 1935, up until the 1990s.

Paleographers and Textual Scholars Date P52 Early and With a Fifty-Year Range

- 100-150 C. H. Roberts
- 100-150 Sir Frederic G. Kenyon
- 100-150 W. Schubart
- 100-150 Sir Harold I. Bell
- 100-150 Adolf Deissmann
- 100-150 E. G. Turner (cautiously)
- 100-150 Ulrich Wilken
- 100-150 W. H. P. Hatch
- 100-200 Daniel B. Wallace
- 100-125: Philip W. Comfort
- 100-150 Bruce M. Metzger
- 125-175 Kurt and Barbara Aland
- 125-175 Pasquale Orsini
- 125-175 Willy Clarysse

The New Textual Scholars Date P52 Later or With a Wider Range

- 81–292 C.E. Don Barker
- 170 C.E. Andreas Schmidt
- 100–225 Brent Nongbri
- 200–300 Michael Gronewald

Andreas Schmidt had redated P52 to 170 C.E., plus or minus 25-years, based on the comparison of two other manuscripts and the redating of P. Egerton 2, which were also paleographically dated that are similar to P52. Thus, "Schmidt redates P52 to ca. 200 based on the fact that its hand parallels that of the Egerton Gospel, which is now thought by some to date closer to ca. 200 based on this feature appearing in a newly published portion of the Egerton Gospel."

Brent Nongbri has found fault with the early dating of P52 [100-125 C.E.] by Philip W. Comfort that the later dating of P52 [170 C.E.] by Andreas Schmidt and with the short range of fifty years by Roberts [100–150 C.E.]. Nongbri has come out against what he believes the narrow dating of the papyri [e.g., 50-year span] on paleographical grounds alone when the papyri have no date within the text of any sort or it has no archaeological evidence. Archaeological evidence can help date manuscripts. For example, Harold P. Scanlin writes, "Around A.D. 70 Qumran was destroyed during the Jewish war and Roman invasion. Thus, assuming that the Dead Sea Scrolls found near the Qumran settlement were the product of that community, then the latest date for the manuscripts hidden in nearby caves is A.D. 70." Of course, there are almost no manuscripts that can be dated on archaeology because there are no circumstances associated with the documents. Moreover, those that may have some archaeological elements, the circumstances are vague or ambiguous. Nongbri rejects all attempts to establish what he feels to be a narrow date for the undated P52 based on paleography alone. Moreover, Nongbri argues that it is circular reasoning when you have paleographic comparisons with other papyri that had themselves also been paleographically dated.

NONGBRI: "I hope that by bringing together the images of the manuscripts cited in previous treatments of P52, as well as some of my own comparanda, I can highlight the uncertainty involved in paleographic dating and encourage caution when using P52 to assess the date (and thus the social setting) of the Fourth Gospel." (Nongbri, p. 27). Bold mine.

NONGBRI: "Paleography is not the most effective method for dating texts, particularly those written in a literary hand." (Nongbri, p. 46) Bold mine.

RESPONSE: Notice what Nongbri just said. This is important because this is being repeated by those following him and this new trend of redating the early papyri. Let me paraphrase Nongbri for you: 'You cannot date any undated papyri document, especially literary ones based on paleography, because it is not the most effective. I [Nongbri] will undermine this whole way of dating papyri by comparing other manuscripts, paleographically, that are dated later using paleography to do so, that I have just condemned in the last sentence.' Nongbri, 'I will dismiss as unsound all attempts to establish a narrow date range for P52 [100–150 C.E.] that are based purely on paleographic grounds. And I will do so based purely on paleographic grounds. I will accept the narrow date range of the later narrowly dated manuscript that I am using to undermine Roberts' so-called narrow date range of P52.'

When Nongbri says that "paleography is not the most effective method," he is also inferring that there must be another more effective preferred way of dating literary undated literary papyri like P52. That is not the case, as Nongbri admits in his own paper that literary papyri, by their very nature, do not contain dates, and almost all have no archaeology associated with them. Then, again, Nongbri uses paleography to undermine the use of paleography. Every textual scholar knows that paleographic dating is conditional and difficult. No one has argued that it is the "most effective method." Every book on textual criticism, paleography, and papyrology makes this patently clear. Not one papyrologist isn't aware of the immense difficulty in finding suitable comparative manuscripts. Of course, there is going to be a measure of subjectivity when one is evaluating the similarities.

Moreover, handwriting comparison is not like DNA comparison and fingerprint comparison. With DNA and fingerprints, we will get an exact, absolute match. Handwriting analysis (comparing) is general in its very nature. We are looking for a general pattern, not that every single letter and style or form must match explicitly in every detail with each other. Roberts and other paleographers put forward certain manuscripts that are clearly and convincingly like P52. This is a high level of proof that P52 dates to 100–150 C.E. This means that we have no reason to doubt; we do not then raise issues because we can cobble together some similar letter(s) from late second century or early third-century C.E.

Again, repetition for emphasis, yes, it will be difficult to assign dates to various paleographical features when we are dealing with literary documents, which is what Bible manuscripts are. Yes, if possible, it would be great to have a corroborating documentary dated material, which we do, on the other side of a biblical papyrus. Yes, if we all lived in a perfect world, we would have dates on every manuscript but it is what it is and while something is "not the most effective" to some, it might be effective to others. It is a far cry from "not the most effective" to being ineffectual. When you have a literary manuscript like P52 that are used to date a literary manuscript, as well as several documentary manuscripts as evidence for P52; then someone comes along with documentary MSS: petitions, a judgment, an invitation, and a receipt to try and redate a longtime established date, this should cause a pause for concern. Sometimes, language is used to convey things beyond the reality of what they are... "not the most effective" and "an unhelpful exercise" becomes a subtle message that is being conveyed beyond the reality of what is because what is difficult is starting to become impossible in the minds of some, who are supporting this new trend of redating the early papyri because it has become popular to do so. They are adding their voices to a growing movement of redating early papyri because the movement has appeared to be taking ground as it becomes successful.

Nongbri suggests that older styles of handwriting might continue much longer than some scholars believed and that a sensible approach must allow for a still wider range of possible dates for the papyrus:

> What emerges from this survey is nothing surprising to papyrologists: paleography is not the most effective method for dating texts, particularly those written in a literary hand. Roberts himself noted this point in his edition of P52. The real problem is thus in the way scholars of the New Testament have used and abused papyrological evidence. I have not radically revised Roberts's work. I have not provided any third-century documentary papyri that are absolute "dead ringers" for the handwriting of P52, and even if I had done so, that would not force us to date P52 at some exact point in the third century. Paleographic evidence does not work that way. What I have done is to show that any serious consideration of the window of possible dates for P52 must include dates in the later second and early third centuries. Thus, P52 cannot be used as evidence to silence other debates about the existence (or non-existence) of the Gospel of John in the first half of the second century. Only a papyrus containing an explicit date or one found in a clear archaeological stratigraphic context could do the work scholars want P52 to do. As it stands now, the papyrological evidence should take a second place to other forms of evidence in addressing debates about the dating of the Fourth Gospel.

One reading Nongbri's article will take note that he does not set a date for P52. In all that Nongbri has written, thought, it would seem that he dates P52 later in his wider range of 100-225 C.E. However, he is willing to concede and accept the cautious words of Roberts, "On the whole, we may accept with some confidence the first half of the second century as the period in which (P52) was most probably written." Nongbri also seems to have no problem with Roberts' theories on possible consequences for the date of John's gospel, "But all we can safely say is that this fragment tends to support those critics who favour an early date (late first to early second century) for the composition of the Gospel rather than those who would still regard it as a work of the middle decades of the second century."

Again, while it might seem to some that Nongbri and Roberts' findings are somewhat similar, we have to consider the consequences of Nongbri's language and demeanor. Just as Nongbri feared conservative evangelicals would cling to the earliest possible part of Roberts' so-called narrow range [100–150 C.E.], so too, Bible critics will cling to the latest possible date of Nongbri's date range of 100-225 C.E. We know the main motivating factor driving Nongbri's research is right in the title of his article, "The Use and Abuse of P52: Papyrological Pitfalls in the Dating of the Fourth Gospel." He is being driven by the fear of a conservative evangelical scholar abusing Roberts' range. The objective should be that we look at the evidence and offer our best conclusion on what the evidence says, regardless of who uses or abuses the findings.

Nongbri's approach in his article was to revisit and compare P52 with the manuscripts used by Roberts and others since, as well as some of his own, to evidence that similar handwriting styles existed before the date of P52 given by Roberts and after that date as well. This sounds like a fair approach, so we will do that here in a later chapter as well. However, we shall tweak the look and the approach.

Nongbri's Methodological Shift and Its Limitations

Brent Nongbri has increasingly argued for caution in assigning specific dates to early Christian manuscripts based solely on paleographic evidence. In his works, including *God's Library* (2018), he recommends supplementing—or in some cases replacing—paleographic dating with codicological analysis and radiocarbon testing. While at first glance this may seem like a more scientific and objective approach, such methods can be misleading or limited in application when removed from the comparative framework that defines paleography.

Radiocarbon dating, for example, is not date-specific to the writing of the manuscript but to the **age of the organic material**—i.e., the papyrus or parchment. This means a manuscript could be written decades *after* the papyrus was produced and processed. Without contextual clues from scribal style or manuscript format, radiocarbon testing provides a **range too broad** to be determinative for literary texts. For instance, a carbon date might place the material between 150–250 C.E., but if the script clearly parallels documents securely dated to 100–125 C.E., such data can **obscure rather than clarify**.

Codicology, the study of the book as a physical artifact, offers valuable insights into binding, format, page layout, and reuse. But Nongbri's growing tendency to lean more heavily on these features, sometimes at the expense of paleographic comparison, risks minimizing the **specific scribal traits** that link undated literary texts to securely dated ones. For example, one might argue that because a scribe used a particular style of hooked apostrophe or punctuation commonly found in the early third century, the entire manuscript must be dated to that period. But this ignores the fact that scribes are individuals, and individual habits or innovations can appear decades earlier in isolated cases.

Furthermore, the strength of paleographic dating lies in its ability to draw **multiple points of comparison** with dated documentary texts. When Nongbri expresses skepticism toward this method, he fails to acknowledge the level of control afforded by manuscript samples with secure provenance, such as those with dated colophons or documentary content. By reducing the weight of this comparative discipline, Nongbri inadvertently undercuts the strongest dating anchors available for manuscripts like P52, which—despite being fragmentary—shares close stylistic kinship with manuscripts dated confidently between 100 and 150 C.E.

In practice, Nongbri's methodology often leads to **inflated date ranges**—not because the manuscript demands it, but because he resists drawing firm conclusions from paleographic likeness. This opens the door to excessive caution that, while academically "safe," results in ambiguity. The very goal of dating—to narrow the field of historical placement—is lost when a method systematically resists closure. Paleography, when used responsibly and in tandem with contextual evidence, remains the most effective means for dating undated Greek New Testament manuscripts.

Expanded Critique of Nongbri's Codicological Dating Approach

Brent Nongbri's dating methodology has gained attention for emphasizing codicological features and radiocarbon testing over traditional paleographic analysis. While his work raises valid questions about assumptions in manuscript dating, his conclusions often overstate the evidential weight of codicological and radiocarbon data, especially when used in isolation or as a primary argument for redating.

Limitations of Codicological Dating

Codicological observations—such as measurements of page dimensions, reconstruction of quire structures, ruling patterns, or binding folds—are valuable for understanding the physical construction and usage of a codex. However, they are subject to significant chronological overlap and regional variation. For example, vertical ruling lines or single-quire formats appear in both second- and third-century manuscripts, and dimensions can be influenced more by practical considerations (e.g., reuse of papyrus) than by time-specific conventions.

Moreover, the absence of certain features (e.g., lack of pagination, marginal notations) cannot be used to exclude an earlier date. P. Oxy. 841 and P. Oxy. 1622, securely dated to the early second century, exhibit varied codicological formats, which show no strict standardization across scribes and locations. Codicology, by nature, offers supporting context but not primary evidence for chronological placement.

Radiocarbon Dating: Useful but Broad and Inexact

Radiocarbon dating, although scientific in nature, provides probabilistic ranges that often span 50 to 150 years. When applied to ancient manuscripts such as P46 or P66, this can place a document anywhere from the late first century to the mid-third century. The raw data must be calibrated and interpreted, and even then, the result reflects when the papyrus plant died—not when the manuscript was written.

For instance, the radiocarbon dating of P46 has produced ranges overlapping with the early to late second century, yet the paleographic evidence places it squarely within the 100–150 C.E. range, as supported by comparisons with P. Oxy. 1622, P. Berol. 9810, and P. Oxy. 841. In these cases, radiocarbon dating may affirm a general chronological range but lacks the specificity required for establishing the fine-grained temporal relationships needed in New Testament textual studies.

Paleography Remains the Most Precise Tool

By contrast, paleography—when applied by seasoned experts and compared against securely dated documentary texts—can often place a manuscript within a 25- to 50-year range. This is especially the case for documents such as P52, where the form of specific letters (e.g., alpha, mu, upsilon, and tau) matches closely with dated papyri from the early second century, such as P. Oxy. 841 (second hand) and P. Berol. 9810. These visual comparisons allow for relatively precise alignment of scribal practices across manuscripts.

Notably, Nongbri himself concedes that paleography provides the clearest basis for dating when dealing with isolated fragments or manuscripts with no internal dates. However, in his analysis of P52, he downplays paleographic concords in favor of theoretical uncertainties. His claim that

P52 could date as late as the third century relies on the broadest outer range of codicological and radiocarbon interpretations, without adequate weight to the consistent early second-century letterforms.

Methodological Caution in Overstating Alternative Dating Techniques

Nongbri's approach often implies that because absolute certainty is impossible, all dating estimates should be held in equal suspicion. This undermines the legitimate discriminating power of paleographic parallels. While no dating method is infallible, the convergence of letterform comparison with securely dated parallels provides a stronger case than general codicological features or radiocarbon ranges. Indeed, when these latter methods contradict or weaken paleographic conclusions, their broader imprecision should be acknowledged as a limitation, not as justification for overturning more precise assessments.

In sum, while codicology and radiocarbon can be useful in a broader analytical framework, they cannot override or displace paleographic analysis when secure visual parallels exist. Nongbri's attempts to revise the dating of P52, P66, or other early Christian codices must be evaluated within this hierarchy of methodological precision.

	Radiocarbon Dating	Paleography	Codicology
Dating Range	Broad	Moderate	Broad
Margin of Error	±40–100 years	± 25–50 years	± 50+ years
Consistency with Dated Examples	Inconsistent	Consistent	Inconsistent
Cross-Regional Applicability	Yes	Yes	Yes

THE P52 PROJECT

CHAPTER 6 Stanley Porter and P52

The revised dating for the P. Egerton 2 continues to carry wide support among some of the new textual scholars. However, Stanley Porter has reviewed the dating of the P. Egerton 2 alongside that of P52; noting that the scholarly consensus dating the former to the turn of the third century and the latter to the first half of the second century was contra-indicated by close paleographic similarities of the two manuscripts. The 1987 redating of the Egerton Papyrus had rested on a comment made by Eric Turner in 1971 (albeit that Turner himself had continued until his death in 1983 to accept a mid-second century date for the Egerton Papyrus), "in the first decade of III AD this practice (of using an apostrophe between two consonants, such as double mutes or double liquids) suddenly becomes extremely common, and then persists." Porter then offers this insight into Turner's comments.

> This was a major factor in pulling the dating of the two manuscripts apart. However, here is what Turner actually says: "In the first decade of iii ad this practice [of using an apostrophe between two consonants, such as double mutes or double liquids] suddenly becomes extremely common and then persists." Note that Turner does not say that the practice does not exist before the third century ad, but that in the first decade it becomes "extremely common" and then "persists."

Porter notes that Turner had advanced several earlier dated examples of the practice from the later second century, and one (BGU III 715.5) dated to 101 CE. Porter proposes that, notwithstanding the discovery of the hooked apostrophe in P. Köln 255, the original editors' proposal of a mid-second century date for the Egerton Papyrus accords better with the paleographic evidence of dated comparator documentary and literary hands for both P52 and this papyrus "the middle of the second century, perhaps tending towards the early part of it."

Porter has also offered us two further comparator early biblical papyri for both texts. He has given us P. Oxy IV 656 (a fragment of Genesis) and P.Vindob. G. 2325 (the Fayum Fragment). Porter presents a wide-ranging analysis of the history and assortment of views amongst papyrologists for the dating and redating of P52 and P. Egerton 2. He then goes on to offer us supporting evidence that Roberts' conclusions that the two are close parallels is correct.

Edward D. Andrews

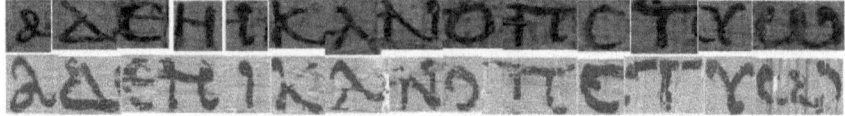

Image P52 (100-150 C.E.) bottm P. Egerton 2 (150 C.E.) top

He further notes, "Nevertheless, there are some differences between the two hands. Roberts had noted early on that the hand of P.Ryl. III 457 (P52) was 'a heavy, rounded and rather elaborate hand,' which 'often uses several strokes to form a single letter ... with a rather clumsy effect.' The scribe also adds 'a small flourish or hook to the end of his strokes.' By comparison, P.Egerton 2 is a less heavy hand with more formal rounded characteristics, but also with what the original editors called 'cursive affinities.'" (Porter, p. 82-3). P52 and P.Egerton 2 are highly unlikely to possess widely separate dates, as well as P52 dating somewhat earlier than P.Egerton 2, say Porter in agreement with Roberts, "on the basis of comparisons and the less formal character of the hand. There is nothing here to dispute this analysis." (p. 83). Porter adds that "Both manuscripts were apparently written before development of the more formal Biblical majuscule style, which began to develop in the late second and early third centuries." (Porter, p 83).

Stanley Porter has also doubted Nongbri's claim that legitimate comparisons are able to be made between P52 and dated documentary papyri of the late second and early third centuries. Nongbri writes, "What is needed, then, is a re-examination of all Roberts's evidence and particularly an update of comparanda, preferably documentary papyri with dates, in order to question New Testament scholars' early and overly specific dating of P52, typified by the recent work of Comfort and Barrett." Porter then goes on to quote the warning from Turner that "[c]onfidence will be strongest when like is compared with like: a documentary hand with another documentary hand, skilful writing with skilful, fast writing with fast. Comparison of book hands with dated documentary hands will be less reliable, the intention of the scribe is different in the two cases. ...; besides, the book-hand style in question may have had a long life." (Porter, pp.79-80)

One of the technical shortcomings of Nongbri's argument lies in his selective reliance on documentary papyri such as P.Bas. 2.43 and P.Ant. 2.78. Both are demonstrably informal hands, written for utilitarian purposes, and lacking the deliberate stylization evident in P52's literary script. P.Bas. 2.43, dated 114 C.E., is a private letter whose cursive tendencies betray a personal, hurried execution—not the practiced consistency expected in a scribe's literary hand. P.Ant. 2.78, likewise, is a receipt dated 127 C.E., bearing irregularities and flourishes that are typical of everyday transactional records. Neither manuscript resembles the careful semi-formal or formal stylization of P52, which aligns far better with literary production standards. By drawing parallels with such dissimilar exemplars, Nongbri undermines the precision of his argument. Paleography, if it is to be meaningful, requires "like to be compared with like," as E. G. Turner reminded us. Yet Nongbri's use of dissimilar documentary papyri masks the true stylistic distance between P52 and his chosen comparanda, raising questions about methodological consistency and the legitimacy of his revised dating framework.

In this, Port makes the astute observation that Nongbri with his 'over skeptical' doggedness to remove any consideration of comparators that do not possess an explicit date, which means the literary texts, that is, the New Testament manuscripts, would be restricted to documentary hands. (Porter, p. 81.) He goes on to argue that Nongbri's suggested late second and third-century manuscript comparisons are in numerous cases fairly different from P52. Porter says that Nongbri is forcing us to place all of our overall attention on a couple to a few specific detailed letter forms without any real thought being given to the overall formation, trajectory and the style of the script. Porter says, "A typological comparison should not focus simply on a single letter or a single formation of a letter. However, a typological comparison can be used when there is a range of letters that have been established within a time period. Comparison of the individual letters of the two manuscripts, P.Ryl. III 457 (P52) and P.Egerton 2, with the sets of letters in both Maunde Thompson's and Turner's representative alphabets indicates what may appear to be a surprising result in the light of recent discussion. Both manuscripts clearly fit comfortably within the second century." (Porter, p. 82).

Then, Porter states that both P52 and P. Egerton 2 "fit comfortably within the second century. There are of course some letters that are similar to those in the third century (as there are some in the first century) but the letters that tend to be given the most individualization, such as alpha, mu and even sigma, appear to be second century." (Porter, p. 82.) Nongbri admits, "In 1977, Eric Turner had the following to say about Roberts's dating of P52: 'I have no evidence to invalidate the first editor's [Robert's] dating to the first half of the second century. But I should echo his warning about the need for caution.'" Porter also draws attention to this fact, "More importantly perhaps is that there have been later papyrologists who have been more cautious, but who have still endorsed Roberts's earlier conclusion, including Eric Turner forty years later." (Porter, p. 77).

Edward D. Andrews

Affirming and Expanding Stanley Porter's Position on P52's Paleographic Date

Stanley Porter's extensive analysis of the Rylands Greek P 457 (P52) manuscript has offered one of the most robust defenses of the early second-century dating originally proposed by C.H. Roberts. Porter's argumentation, founded upon both methodological clarity and textual nuance, avoids speculative extremes while upholding paleography as the primary and most appropriate tool for assigning a relative date to such fragmentary evidence. His view finds natural alignment with the trajectory of this present study, and further augmentation of his claims can both reinforce the early dating of P52 and clarify the methodological issues that have become points of contention in recent scholarly literature.

The Paleographic Priority and Its Methodological Rigor

Porter argues that paleographic analysis remains the most reliable means for dating undated Greek literary papyri, particularly when comparative samples are abundant and the manuscript in question contains sufficient data for evaluating handwriting features. In contrast to more speculative or generalized approaches (such as codicology or radiocarbon dating), paleography provides a direct basis for comparison, grounded in empirical similarities of letter formation, ductus, and stylistic tendencies observable across securely dated papyri.

He emphasizes that P52's script bears striking resemblance to a specific group of Roman-period literary hands from the late first and early second centuries. As shown in his analysis, comparisons to manuscripts such as P. Berol. 9810 (early 2nd century), P. Oxy. 841 (second hand; 125–150 C.E.), and P. Oxy. 1622 (117–138 C.E.) confirm the consistency of P52 with early second-century hands. Porter points to the slanted epsilon, the rounded and open theta, and the square-ish omicron—all characteristics visible in P52 and mirrored in early second-century comparanda.

His core methodological stance—that paleography is best understood as a comparative, rather than an absolute, science—resonates with this project's broader evaluation. Paleography, when executed through close analysis of dated control texts, avoids the generalizations that plague codicological or radiocarbon-centered efforts. Porter's view corrects the misrepresentation that paleographic dating is purely subjective; he rightly observes that when properly applied to literary hands of this period, the degree of precision achievable is often within a 50-year window—sufficient for placing P52 in the early second century with high confidence.

The Fallacy of Overturning Consensus Without New Paleographic Data

Another point where Porter's reasoning deserves emphasis is in his rebuttal to the redating attempts by Brent Nongbri and others. These revisionist efforts often appeal to codicological or historical-theological assumptions rather than to fresh paleographic observations. Porter is clear: no one has presented new paleographic data that would materially alter the original comparisons made by Roberts or those corroborated by later scholars like Bell, Kenyon, or Turner.

This is a critical observation. Nongbri, for example, shifts the conversation toward the theological significance of assigning a late first- or early second-century date to a Gospel fragment, implying that apologetic motives may have driven the early dating. Yet as Porter argues, such insinuations are irrelevant to the technical paleographic analysis. Even if apologists found P52's early date advantageous, that in no way undermines the actual letterform evidence, especially when such evidence is evaluated against neutral control manuscripts dated by independent external means.

Rather than attempting to discredit the paleographic consensus by means of ancillary disciplines, Porter calls for careful empirical work within paleography itself. In this, he sets the standard for methodological integrity—an approach this present study seeks to emulate.

Codicology and Radiocarbon: Supporting Roles, Not Primary Tools

While Porter acknowledges that codicological and radiocarbon data can sometimes provide helpful supporting information, he is clear in maintaining their secondary role when compared to paleographic analysis. This distinction is particularly relevant in light of Nongbri's more recent strategy of emphasizing codicological features—such as codex size, margin breadth, or text block format—as decisive dating tools.

Porter rightly resists this trend. Codicology may tell us something about book production practices, but it is rarely sufficient for precise dating. Many physical features of manuscripts persisted for decades or even centuries across different regions. For example, the shift from scroll to codex among Christian communities is evident, but it occurred gradually and with regional variance. As such, a manuscript's codicological profile may confirm that it fits within a general historical trend (e.g., second-century Christian codex culture), but it cannot provide the kind of chronological precision that paleographic letterform comparisons allow.

Radiocarbon analysis, likewise, offers broad date ranges that are often too imprecise to resolve the fine distinctions necessary for fragment-level dating. A radiocarbon result for a papyrus sheet may yield a calibrated date range spanning up to a century or more, rendering it essentially useless for determining whether P52 should be dated to 110 C.E. or 180 C.E.—a distinction crucial in historical theology and textual criticism. Porter's skepticism about using radiocarbon analysis to overturn paleographic consensus is, therefore, both warranted and prudent.

Expanding the Framework: Porter's Contribution to Textual Trajectory

While Porter's primary focus is on paleographic methodology, his observations implicitly support an even broader conclusion—namely, that the early second-century date of P52 places it well within the window of active textual transmission of the Fourth Gospel in Egypt. The manuscript's physical features (single column layout, codex form, clear literary script) align with early Christian preferences for codex usage, and the text itself—John 18:31–33, 37–38—reflects a section of the Gospel known to have circulated widely among early communities.

Porter is not simply affirming an early date for the sake of chronological taxonomy; rather, he is contributing to the overall picture of how and when the Gospel of John gained literary currency. If P52 indeed dates to around 125 C.E., as Porter and this study maintain, it implies that John's Gospel was already composed, copied, and distributed by that time—likely by the beginning of the second century at the latest.

Moreover, Porter's defense of Roberts' date is not a nostalgic appeal to an outdated opinion but a recognition that Roberts used a methodologically sound approach based on carefully chosen comparative hands. Subsequent scholars, including E.G. Turner, Bruce Metzger, and Comfort & Barrett, have affirmed and refined Roberts' estimate, and Porter stands in that same stream of disciplined scholarship. His rejection of attempts to force a much later dating on P52—without producing any manuscript with letterforms more closely resembling P52 dated to the later second or third centuries—is both logical and fair.

Harmonizing Porter's Approach with Current Findings

This present work extends Porter's logic by providing photographic overlays and direct visual comparisons between P52 and its closest dated parallels, reaffirming the strength of his paleographic conclusions. These visual aids—such as the overlays of epsilon and mu in P52 and P. Oxy. 1622—provide empirical substantiation of the affinities Porter identified through descriptive analysis. Rather than abstract or generalized comparison, these images offer concrete, verifiable parallels that support the early dating thesis.

Furthermore, Porter's insistence that no new paleographic data has been offered to justify redating P52 remains unchallenged. The attempt by Nongbri to utilize codicological data such as format and layout, or sociological trends regarding Gospel circulation, does not amount to a reassessment of P52's handwriting itself. Unless a manuscript emerges with close paleographic resemblance to P52 and a secure late date, Porter's early dating remains the most rational and supported conclusion.

Conclusion

Stanley Porter's defense of the early second-century date for P52 stands as one of the most methodologically coherent and textually grounded positions in the field. His affirmation of Roberts' original conclusions is not an uncritical repetition of past scholarship but a reinforcement rooted in empirical paleographic comparison, caution against methodological overreach, and a strong awareness of the limitations of alternative approaches. This present project finds strong alignment with Porter's reasoning and seeks to build upon his contribution by offering additional visual, codicological, and paleographic data that substantiate the same conclusion: P52 belongs to the early part of the second century, reinforcing the early circulation and textual stability of the Gospel of John.

Edward D. Andrews

CHAPTER 7 Don Barker and P52

I should note that Dr. Don Barker, a Papyrologist at Macquarie University, has been my sounding board while I have worked on this book. I have had three scholars who have the position of dating P52 with a wider range and later date range who have helped me to find sources and also have back and forth discussion by email or Messenger: papyrologist Dr. Don Parker, Senior translator of the NASB, since 1992 Dr. Don Wilkins, and papyrologist Dr. Elijah Hixon.

Barker states his concerns as, "The narrow dating of some of the early New Testament papyri and the methodological approach that is used must be brought into question in the light of the acknowledged difficulties with palaeographical dating and especially the use of assigned dated literary papyri." (Barker, p. 571). Barker and some others have a totally different approach to dating the New Testament papyri. Over the past few years, they have drawn on the idea of what is known as "graphic stream," which was developed by Guglielmo Cavallo. They are not in favor of comparing the forms of letters from undated literary papyri with dated documentary papyri. Rather, Barker and company feel that the handwriting style that needs to be dated should first be placed in a "graphic stream," which is representative of the entire period of a specific handwriting style.

For example, the Roman Uncial can run from 30 B.C. to around 200, even for some 300 C.E. Decorated Rounded Uncial ran from the first century B.C.E. to the end of the first century C.E., so says Schubart. On the other hand, Turner and others felt that it extended to the end of the second century C.E. Another graphic stream would be the Biblical Uncial or Biblical Majuscule, which could be said to run from the first century C.E. to the late 4th century. Another example would be the Severe Style, which has manuscript representatives from the first century to the early fourth century C.E. On the Biblical uncial Comfort writes, "G. Cavallo, in his majesterial work, Richerche sulla Maiuscola Biblica, makes a strong case for the style known as Biblical Uncial taking definitive shape in the middle to late second century AD. In order to justify this dating, he drew upon a few significant manuscripts whose dates are fairly well established.

On placing the manuscript under consideration in a specific graphic stream, Barker writes, "The way that individual letters are formed within these graphic streams is secondary to the overall style of the script." (Barker, p. 572) Barker, in his article, The Dating of New Testament Papyri, reviews the manuscripts that have been compared to P52, and the date ranges that have been offered over the years. Barker says of P52 "the graphic stream that

P.Ryl. 457 represents is attested in the first century AD and onwards. It is a round block script that has cursive letter formations written with a fluid ductus, the two oblique middle strokes of the mu are combined to form a dish shape, omega and upsilon are generally formed with loops, epsilon has an extended middle hastas and the obliques of lamda, upsilon, mu and delta are often written with a curl at the top." (Barker, p. 574). Barker goes on to say,

> Variations occur within this graphic stream due to the proficiency of the scribe, writing speed, individual stylistic preferences and document type. The majority of the following documents are documentary and many need to be viewed from the perspective of how the scribe might write a more formal manuscript such as a book. Dated examples for the P.Ryl. 457 stream are: P.Oxy. 3466 (81– 96), P.Fay. 110 (94), P.Oxy. 3016 (148), P.Mich. inv.5366 (152), P.Oxy. 4060 (159–163), P.Amh. 78 (184), P.Oxy. 2968 (190), P.Oxy. 3614 (200), P.Mich. inv.2789 a+b(203–206), P.Oxy. 3694 (2018–225), P.Oxy. 3183 (292). The question is, where does P.Ryl. 457 fit in this continuum? As can be observed, the graphic stream in which P.Ryl. 457 is to be located appears to have great holding power in its letter formation (hence Turner's II, Schmidt's early III). (Barker, p. 574). – Bold mine.

These dated documentary manuscripts ranging from P.Oxy. 3466 (81-96 C.E.) to P.Oxy.3183 (292 C.E.), that is, a range of 81–292 C.E. These dated documentary manuscripts include all the later manuscripts proposed by Brent Nongbri as well as E. G. Turner and the P.Fayum 110 (94 CE) from C.H. Roberts's original study back in 1935. However, Barker rejects all of the other manuscripts that Roberts compared to P52, and those he had corresponded with as well, which would include P. Flor 1. 1 (153 CE). As can be seen from the quote above, Barker claims that the form of the letters within this the graphic stream "appears to have great holding power" and suggests that it is …

> Consequently it is difficult to place P.Ryl. 457 in a very narrow time period. When the general style and individual letter features are kept in close connection and keeping in mind how a scribe writing a documentary text may write a literary text differently, it would seem, from the above dated manuscripts, that a date of II or III could be assigned to P.Ryl. 457. This may be unsatisfactory for those who would like to locate P.Ryl. 457 in a narrower time frame but the palaeographical evidence will not allow it.

Don Barker, on Facebook messenger, "It is a circular argument when you use one undated (i.e., there's no internal evidence in the MSS for a date such as an Emperor's name or some other official of which we know) manuscript to date another manuscript. What we need is an internally dated MSS as comparanda (compared)."

What is it about literary documents that enable the paleographer to section out different hands to different time periods: Ptolemaic period, Roman period, Byzantine period? More specifically, we have, as was explained above, the Roman Uncial, the Decorated Rounded Uncial, the Biblical Uncial or Biblical Majuscule, and the Severe Style. Professional or semi-professional scribes largely do literary documents. When we think about the dating of P52 that now has almost a century behind it (since 1935) with leading paleographers and papyrologists, both Nongbri and Barker are arguing what is possible and not even considering what is probable, which seems to be more clinging to skepticism when it comes to matters of Scripture, that is, postmodernism. The difficulty in dating undated literary manuscripts is well known and accepted by everyone. No one has argued as Nongbri has suggested that paleographical dating is the "most effective method." Every book on textual criticism and paleography makes this patently clear. There is not one papyrologist who isn't aware of the immense difficulty in finding suitable comparative manuscripts. Of course, there is going to be a measure of subjectivity when one is evaluating the similarities. Again, yes, there it is going to be difficult to assign dates to various paleographical features when we are dealing with literary documents, which is what Bible manuscripts are. Yes, if it would be great to have corroborating documentary dated manuscripts if possible, which we do have for P52. It is a far cry from "not the most effective" to being ineffectual.

Evaluating and Responding to Don Barker's Reassessment of P52's Paleographic Date

Don Barker has proposed a notable reassessment of the dating of Papyrus P52 (Rylands Greek P. 457), suggesting that the traditionally accepted early second-century date—especially that of C.H. Roberts (100–150 C.E.)—might be premature or overconfident. Barker's analysis invites critical scrutiny, particularly in how it reorients the methodology by shifting weight away from rigorous paleographic comparison toward a broader, sometimes more ambiguous, codicological and visual typology approach. While his caution is commendable, his conclusions lack sufficient evidentiary anchoring, particularly in comparative detail, which undercuts the force of his arguments. The following response aims to engage Barker's central claims directly and provide a fuller defense of the early dating of P52 within the broader framework of second-century papyrology and Christian book production.

THE P52 PROJECT

1. The Core of Barker's Challenge: A Cautionary Tone on Paleographic Precision

Barker's main objection rests on the premise that paleography, by nature, yields wide dating windows and is prone to interpretive bias. He is not incorrect in identifying that paleographic dating is an art as much as it is a science. However, Barker moves from this observation to an implicit skepticism that unduly minimizes paleography's long-standing methodological reliability. Rather than bolstering his case with new evidence, Barker tends to rely on general uncertainty to lower the evidentiary value of the early dating. His tone is more a critique of confidence than of method—yet the paleographic comparisons between P52 and securely dated literary hands such as P. Oxy. 841, P. Berol. 9810, and P. Egerton 1 remain robust and documented.

While Barker warns that one cannot definitively assign P52 to a precise decade (a caution we would agree with), his position then opens the door to an expanded dating range (late second to even third century), which lacks a counterweight of equally rigorous comparative examples. If anything, Barker's analysis would benefit from exactly the kind of detailed letterform-by-letterform comparison that Roberts, Comfort, and others have undertaken—an exercise that would either confirm or disconfirm the plausibility of such a later dating.

2. Roberts's Methodology Still Holds Weight

Barker downplays the comparative strategy used by C.H. Roberts in his original 1935 publication. However, Roberts employed the best methodological practice of his day—analyzing specific letterforms (such as alpha, delta, epsilon, mu, nu, omega, and tau) and matching them against papyri with relatively secure dating. His reference to P. Fay. 110 (94 C.E.), P. Oxy. 1622 (117–138 C.E.), and P. Berol. 9810 (early second century) showed stylistic overlap with the P52 hand. These are not casual analogies—they are typological parallels grounded in paleographic minutiae. Barker offers little in the way of disproof of these affinities; his skepticism is more tonal than evidentiary.

Furthermore, Roberts was well aware of the limitations of paleography, as his own cautions demonstrate. Yet the clustering of analogs to P52 within the first half of the second century is statistically and typologically significant. Barker's suggestion that the fragment could just as plausibly date to the late second or early third century fails to engage with the cumulative weight of those early analogs.

3. Barker's Presentation of "Visual Style" Is Underdeveloped

One of Barker's contributions is his emphasis on the "visual style" of manuscripts rather than simply discrete letterform comparisons. He draws attention to the overall appearance of hand, spacing, and execution. While this can be helpful, it is only diagnostically useful when paired with precise, comparative illustrations—and these are notably sparse in his publications. A generalized visual impression cannot replace granular data in paleographic assessment. The early dating of P52 rests not on vague impressions but on documented letterform analogs, many of which have been reevaluated and reaffirmed by later scholars (Comfort, Orsini, Clarysse, Turner).

Moreover, Barker's recontextualization of visual similarities, such as comparisons with P. Oxy. 291 (mid-second century), are less specific than necessary for the degree of chronological revision he suggests. His hesitancy to date P52 early is not necessarily grounded in a contradiction of the data but rather in an elevation of perceived paleographic imprecision.

4. The Implausibility of a Late Second-Century Christian Codex Format

Barker's openness to a late second-century or even early third-century dating does not fully grapple with the codicological context of P52. This fragment is part of a codex—a format widely, and almost uniquely, adopted by early Christians well before it became popular in the broader literary culture of the Greco-Roman world. If Barker is correct that P52 belongs to a much later period, it would place this small fragment at the tail-end of the codex's distinctive early Christian identity and into an era when codices were more widely used across other domains. But P52 does not reflect the layout sophistication of later Christian codices (e.g., P45, P46); rather, it preserves the simple format of a primitive codex, reinforcing its place in an earlier phase of Christian book production, possibly even from an era when the codex was still a cultural marker of Christian identity.

Therefore, Barker's late dating not only minimizes the strong paleographic parallels but also neglects the codicological anomaly his theory would produce. The codex format, in its primitive simplicity and physical makeup in P52, fits more logically within the 100–150 C.E. range rather than a later date when codex production had become more standardized and widely adopted beyond the Christian community.

5. Radiocarbon Dating Is Not a Practical Option for P52

Barker occasionally hints at the potential of radiocarbon dating as a corrective to paleographic uncertainty. But P52's tiny size precludes this possibility. The fragment is too valuable—and too small—to be subjected to destructive analysis. As such, the suggestion of radiocarbon dating remains more theoretical than actionable. Paleography, for better or worse, remains the best and only available method. Barker's critique would carry more weight if he proposed a viable alternative, but at present, his approach dismantles the strongest evidence (paleography) without supplying a replacement of equivalent diagnostic strength.

Moreover, even when radiocarbon dating is available, it offers date ranges that are often broader than paleographic ones. For example, the Dead Sea Scrolls exhibit ranges of ±50 years, which makes them useful in conjunction with paleography, not in replacement of it. Codicological features and radiocarbon dating alone cannot provide the granular precision that paleography can when cross-referenced with securely dated papyri. This reinforces the methodological robustness of the earlier dating assigned to P52 by Roberts and reaffirmed by Comfort and others.

6. Comfort's Defense as a Counterweight

Philip Comfort's extensive reassessment of P52 and the entire papyrological corpus, particularly in his volume *The Text of the Earliest New Testament Greek Manuscripts*, directly challenges Barker's hesitancy. Comfort offers dozens of photographic comparisons, revisiting the original manuscripts cited by Roberts and adding newly discovered ones. His paleographic work reaffirms the early second-century dating, narrowing the range to 100–125 C.E. with greater precision than earlier scholarship. Comfort's paleography is grounded in the same manuscript tradition Barker references, yet he comes to a different conclusion precisely because of the comparative detail Barker avoids. Comfort's commitment to direct letterform matching—μ, υ, ω, α, and others—stands as a methodological contrast to Barker's more impressionistic critique.

It is worth noting that Barker does not offer a robust rebuttal to Comfort's reevaluation. Instead, his work seems to function more as a general caution against dating certainty rather than a detailed, item-by-item reanalysis. The lack of substantive counterexamples or detailed comparisons undermines Barker's argument.

Conclusion

Barker's contribution to the conversation surrounding P52 reflects a valuable academic caution, but it ultimately lacks the comparative specificity required to overturn the strong case for an early second-century date. His appeal to general uncertainties in paleographic method, along with unverified codicological possibilities and theoretical radiocarbon alternatives, does not constitute sufficient warrant to abandon the detailed, analog-driven analysis of Roberts, Comfort, and others. P52 remains most convincingly dated to 100–150 C.E., supported by clear typological parallels, contextual fit within early Christian codex culture, and paleographic consistency with securely dated literary hands. While methodological humility is always needed, it must not come at the expense of data-driven conclusions. P52's early date remains the best-supported and most responsible scholarly position.

CHAPTER 8 Pasquale Orsini and Willy Clarysse and P52

Pasquale Orsini is an Italian paleographer, librarian, and Professor from Università di Catania-Siracusa. Willy Clarysse, KU Leuven, Department of Ancient History, Emeritus. Studies Ancient History, Greek Epigraphy, and Hellenistic History.

Pasquale Orsini and Willy Clarysse are also onboard with the "graphic stream" approach that was mentioned in our previous chapter. They have applied the approach in their review as they dated all New Testament manuscripts that had been dated before the 350 C.E., which would include P52. As has been stated herein many times, none of the papyri, nor the parchments for that matter, have explicit dates. Therefore, Orsini and Clarysse suggested that manuscript comparisons for such paleographic dating must be made only with hands that are similar to each other.

However, unlike Don Barker, Orsini and Clarysse have a classification of hands that conform strictly to the typology of Hellenistic Greek styles of handwriting, which Guglielmo Cavallo developed. They applied his categorization of hands into 'styles', 'stylistic classes', or 'graphic types.' Orsini and Clarysse suggest dates for NT papyri that are often somewhat later than the dates in the Nestle-Aland lists. (Orsini, p. 466) The dates of the NT papyri by Orsini and Clarysse are significantly later than those set by Comfort and Barrett. (Orsini, p. 445) A sign of the disparity in this new camp of paleographers and papyrologists is that they criticize Don Barker because his date range of 81–292 C.E. is too early for them. (Orsini, p. 460.) The date range that they have set for the NT papyri is a maximum of 100 years, but generally 50 years. However, there are even cases when they suggest purely paleographically dates for some of the early papyri P46, P95, P64+67) within a 25-year range. (Orsini, p. 470)

Orsini and Clarysse, in their paper, Early New Testament Manuscripts and Their Dates, say that the manuscripts put forward by Comfort and Barrett in their dating of P52 are "inappropriate" (Orsini, p. 462), while at the same time they accept and approve of the assessment of the papyrological dating of Nongbri, which he adopted from Grenfell, Hunt and Roberts, Orsini and Clarysse neglect to cite Nongbri's specific study of P52, including his manuscripts used in his comparison, nor those by Barker as well with his graphic stream.

Image PSI V 446, the official decree of the Prefect Petronio Mamertino dated September 5 133/136 C.E.

Of all the papyri used by Roberts and those he interacted with Orsini and Clarysse go against Barker and uphold Kenyon's proposed dated parallel, P. Flor 1. 1 (153 C.E.) as corresponding to the same "Round Chancery Script" graphic type as P52. (Orsini, p. 458.) There are two addition manuscripts that Orsini and Clarysse compared to P52, PSI V 446, the official decree of the Prefect Petronio Mamertino dated September 5 133/136 C.E.; and P. Fayum 87, a municipal receipt, which has been dated to 156 C.E. (Orsini, p. 462.) They have also taken note of the similarities between P52 and P104, which they have dated to 100–200 CE.

THE P52 PROJECT

Image Papyrus 104 (P104) Dated to the beginning of the second century C.E. by Comfort and Barrett

On P104 Dirk Jongkind,

A lot has happened since then [1935/Roberts] in the study of Greek palaeography and with the increase in readily available collections of digital images and refined classification one would assume that the experts are able to form an even more informed opinion now than they were in the 1930s. A 2012 article by Orsini and Clarysse provides exactly this re-evaluation. Their method is solid and responsible, both scholars have a tremendous track record, and in general I don't find much to disagree with, even though in some of the finer distinctions Orsini and Clarysse make I cannot always follow them. Their evaluation of the date is not far off from what Roberts came up with in giving the range 125-175 for P52. So is P52 still the earliest fragment of the New Testament?

Possibly, but looking through the results presented by Orsini and Clarysse there is another candidate, P104, an interesting fragment of Matthew 21, published in 1997. This papyrus receives a date 100-200. Some particular scripts are easier to pin down than others and that is why P104 has a span of a century, whilst P52 only half a century. So we have P52 and P104 both dated by a range that has its median in the centre of the second century (it may be earlier, it may be later). So what is the oldest manuscript? Well, there are two candidates, P52 of John 18, and P104 of Matthew 21; the former oldest manuscript.

On P104, Comfort and Barrett write,

The editor (J. D. Thomas) dates this fragment to the late second century, while noting that the hand is indeed "early." The question is: how early? The handwriting is carefully executed in what could be called the Roman uncial with a rounded, decorated style. In this style, there is a conscious effort to round letters and to finish every vertical stroke with a serif or decorated roundel. Schubart (naming this style zierstil) thought this style was current from the last century of the Ptolemaic period (first century B.C.) to the end of the first century A.D. Others, such as Turner, saw it as extending to the end of the second century or early third. Turner cited P. Oxy. 3030 (A.D. 207) as an example. But P. Oxy. 3030 is a mixture of zierstil and other forms. It is not a good comparison to P104. Thomas makes some comparisons between P104 and P. Oxy. 3523 (= P90), but I think the Matthew fragment (P104) is more elegant and earlier. In my opinion, P104 is earlier than P90 (John) and all the other late second-century biblical manuscripts displaying a similar style—namely P. Antinoopolis 7 (Psalms), P. Gr Bib g. 5 (Psalms), P. Oxy. 1074 (Exodus), and P32 (Titus). The hand of P104 is more rigid and ornate, reflecting the earlier Roman uncial style of the Ptolemaic period.

When we look for other comparable manuscripts to help us date P104, one can see similarities with P. Oxy. 454 + PSI 119, dated quite solidly to the mid-second century, and with P. Oxy. 2743, P. Oxy. 3009, and P. Oxy. 3010 (each assigned to the second century). However, P104 bears even greater morphological likeness to three manuscripts dated to the first/second century. The first is P. Berolinenses 6845, the second is PSI 1213, and the third is P. Oxy. 4301, which is probably the work of the same scribe who produced PSI 1213.5 PSI 1213 and P. Oxy. 4301 are the nearest matches to P104 (note especially the formation and/or decoration of the following letters: epsilon, iota, lambda, mu, nu, and rho). The editor of P. Oxy. 4301 dates this manuscript to the late first/early second century. P104 seems to belong to the same period. If this is true, it is the earliest New Testament manuscript. If the date is pushed back to early/middle second century (the scribe may have been an older man working in an earlier style), then P104 is among the earliest of the New Testament manuscripts.

Thus, we have Orsini and Clarysse setting the date range for P52 to 125 – 175 C.E. This range is in alignment with the "mid-second century" set by Stanley Porter. It falls within the range set by Roberts (100–150 C.E.). The bottom end of their range is with the range of Comfort and Barrett (100 – 125 C.E.). However, the fifty-year range is far narrower than what Barker or Nongbri would recommend, but it lands in Barker's range of 81–292 C.E. What gets a bit confusing is why Orsini and Clarysse would close out their article by stating P52, P90, and P104 "probably all [date to] the second half of the second century." (Orsini, p. 466)

Evaluating the Orsini-Clarysse Reassessment: A Defense of the Early Paleographic Dating of P52

Pasquale Orsini and Willy Clarysse represent two of the more methodologically conservative voices in recent paleographical discourse. Their approach—especially as applied to New Testament papyri—prioritizes typological categorization over isolated visual correspondence, effectively shifting the focus from individual letterform matching to overarching scribal tendencies. In their joint paper, "Early New Testament Manuscripts and Their Dates: A Critique of Theological Palaeography" (2012), they offered one of the most direct challenges to the traditional early dating of P52, urging a reconsideration of its paleographic assessment. Their re-dating proposal places P52 in the range of 175–225 C.E., nearly a full century later than the earliest estimates proposed by C.H. Roberts and affirmed by other prominent paleographers such as Comfort, Kenyon, Bell, Schubart, and Hatch.

This section will provide a critical response to Orsini and Clarysse's key methodological and substantive claims, defending the traditional early dating of P52 (110–150 C.E.) and reinforcing the merits of comparative paleographic analysis when done with care and awareness of scribal context. We will engage their typological classification system, assess their appeal to documentary overlap, and re-express the logic behind the earlier dating of P52 by bringing codicological and letterform evidence into sharper focus.

1. The Typological Approach of Orsini and Clarysse

Orsini and Clarysse propose a three-fold typology of Greek handwriting styles used in early Christian literature: the Documentary, the Literary, and the Reformed Documentary. P52, they argue, belongs to the Reformed Documentary type, which combines elements of the informal documentary hand (found in mundane business or legal texts) with some features of book hand styles. Their core contention is that this type flourished not in the first half of the second century, but more prominently in the late second and early third centuries.

However, this approach faces significant challenges. First, their typology, while offering a useful heuristic, is overly rigid when applied to manuscripts like P52 that do not cleanly conform to fixed categories. The lines between book hands and reformed documentary scripts are fluid, especially in provincial or non-scriptorium contexts. Early Christian scribes—working independently or in informal Christian communities—would not necessarily follow the scriptorial stylizations of formal Greco-Roman literary production. By acknowledging that P52 lacks ornamentation and represents a functional transcription, Orsini and Clarysse inadvertently highlight its potential origin in the earlier, more transitional phase of Christian scribal culture.

Further, their conclusion that P52 cannot be dated earlier than 175 C.E. presumes a homogenous trajectory of scribal development and fails to adequately account for the regional variability and idiosyncrasies among early Christian papyri. Scribal training varied dramatically between Roman, Alexandrian, and provincial settings. The earliest Christian communities in Egypt likely lacked the institutional infrastructure of a formal scriptorium, which would produce the polished literary hands seen in later codices. Thus, what Orsini and Clarysse call a "reformed documentary hand" may actually represent a locally emergent hybrid style still situated well within the early second century.

2. Comparative Paleography: The Importance of Securely Dated Parallels

The traditional dating of P52 was based on rigorous paleographic comparison by C.H. Roberts, who consulted several securely dated papyri, such as:

- P. Oxy. 841 (second hand; 125–150 C.E.)
- P. Berol. 9810 (early second century)
- P. Egerton 2 (ca. 125 C.E.)
- P. Fayum 110 (94 C.E.)
- P. Oxy. 1622 (117–138 C.E.)

When juxtaposed with these dated comparanda, P52 exhibits clear and sustained similarities in letterforms—particularly in its **mu, tau, epsilon**, and **upsilon**—that are best placed within a 110–150 C.E. window. It is methodologically flawed to dismiss the weight of such comparative data, especially when the comparanda themselves come from secure archaeological contexts or from dated colophons.

Orsini and Clarysse's reluctance to draw fine-grained comparisons downplays the core method of paleography, which necessarily involves comparing form, ductus, stroke order, and curvature across texts. While letterform comparison must be done cautiously, its wholesale dismissal in favor of generalized typologies undermines the precision paleographers have achieved through over a century of analysis. The more measured response is to retain the comparative approach while recognizing its limits—exactly what Roberts, Turner, and Comfort did.

3. The Codex Format as Chronological Evidence

Another key feature of P52 is its codex format, evident from the alignment of letters and surviving page layout. Codices began to appear among Christians as early as the late first century, and by the second century had become the preferred format for Christian texts. While the codex itself is not a precise dating tool, it corroborates an early second-century date when considered alongside paleographical evidence.

Clarysse and Orsini seem to discount the codex form as a chronological indicator, perhaps due to its longer use span. But its presence in P52 aligns well with the increasing Christian adoption of the codex during the early second century, a trend observed in **P. Egerton 2**, **P. Oxy. 405**, and **P. Oxy. 4009**, all securely dated to the early or mid-second century. In this context, P52's format becomes part of a converging line of evidence.

4. Fragment Size and the "Late Reuse" Hypothesis

A minor but worth-addressing point raised by Orsini and Clarysse relates to the fragmentary nature of P52. They propose that such fragments may reflect the result of reuse or discard, possibly later than the original writing date. However, this line of reasoning adds layers of speculation without substantial gain in dating precision.

Roberts and later Comfort have argued that the wear, fiber breaks, and general condition of P52 point toward genuine use and discard rather than a curated, long-lived circulation. The papyrus is not part of a palimpsest or part of a larger document whose reuse would necessarily demand a much later date. Its isolated state and limited textual content are consistent with early Christian usage and discard patterns rather than later reuse.

5. Counterbalancing the Conservative Caution

One of the primary motivations behind Orsini and Clarysse's critique is to temper what they perceive as "theological paleography"—a tendency to force early dates onto New Testament manuscripts in support of apologetic aims. While the concern for objectivity is valid, it must be equally applied. There is a risk of overcorrection, wherein skepticism replaces careful evaluation.

The early dating of P52 is not a theological maneuver. It is based on multiple lines of paleographic evidence, all converging within the 110–150 C.E. window. The earliest possible dates are supported by parallel analysis with papyri that bear dated colophons or come from archaeologically verifiable layers. To re-date P52 to 200 C.E. without comparably strong evidence introduces unnecessary doubt and undermines well-established methodologies in the field.

Furthermore, dating P52 earlier does not entail the assumption that it is the autographic manuscript or even first-generation. Rather, it shows that the Gospel of John was copied in Egypt no later than the mid-second century, requiring prior circulation of the text and its recognition among Christian communities by that time.

---

6. The Broader Paleographic Consensus

Though Orsini and Clarysse are respected scholars, their redating of P52 has not achieved wide adoption. Many paleographers, including those who follow a cautious approach, continue to affirm an early second-century date. Notable among them:

- **C.H. Roberts (110–150 C.E.)**
- **Philip W. Comfort (100–125 C.E.)**
- **Sir Harold Bell**
- **E.G. Turner (with mild reservations)**
- **W.H.P. Hatch**
- **Ulrich Wilcken**

Even the Alands placed P52 between 125–175 C.E., and Daniel Wallace has affirmed a date range of 100–200 C.E., still overlapping significantly with Roberts and Comfort. Orsini and Clarysse's view—175–225 C.E.—sits at the edge of this spectrum and depends on a rejection of earlier comparative methodologies that remain valid when carefully applied.

7. Conclusion: A Layered and Disciplined Defense

Pasquale Orsini and Willy Clarysse have made a meaningful contribution to the conversation about P52 by highlighting methodological concerns and urging caution. However, their rejection of the early dating is not supported by a stronger body of evidence—only by a different interpretive posture. When the full range of paleographic, codicological, and comparative data is considered, the weight of the evidence supports the traditional view: P52 was likely written between 110 and 150 C.E., no later than 175 C.E. at the outer bound.

Thus, their model must be viewed not as a refutation but as a conservative recalibration—one that should be weighed alongside, not in opposition to, the paleographic consensus. It is premature to abandon Roberts' or Comfort's conclusions in favor of a narrower typological system that downplays letterform comparison and overrelies on typology.

Edward D. Andrews

CHAPTER 9 Elijah Hixon and P52

Elijah Hixson (Ph.D., University of Edinburgh) is a junior research associate in New Testament Text and Language at Tyndale House, Cambridge, and author of Scribal Habits in Sixth-Century Greek Purple Codices.

Elijah Hixon CHAPTER 5 DATING MYTHS PART ONE How We Determine the Age of Manuscripts from the book (Myths and Mistakes In New Testament Textual Criticism), an advocate of a late date for P52 (third century).

Elijah Hixson's Claim:

"P52 does not and cannot offer definitive proof that John's Gospel is a first-century composition by an eyewitness. Even if P52 was written in the afternoon of April 26, AD 125 (it wasn't), it would prove only that sections from John 18 were in Egypt by AD 125. Technically, such a date does not prove that John's Gospel was in its 'final' (canonical) form by then, nor does it prove that the text it contains is any more than a few months old. An early date of P52 might render these possibilities unlikely—even extremely unlikely—but it cannot disprove them."

Response:

This line of argument is a textbook example of a strawman fallacy. Hixson criticizes a claim that conservative scholars—especially those who advocate for an early date for P52—never actually make. No one asserts that P52 alone offers "definitive proof" of Johannine authorship or a finalized canon. Rather, P52 contributes to a cumulative case already grounded in strong internal and external evidence for apostolic authorship and a first-century date. Paleography, while not absolute, adds corroborative value—not categorical proof—to the broader scholarly consensus that the Gospel of John was written late in the first century by the apostle John.

By asserting that a precise date for P52 fails to prove authorship or canonical status, Hixson effectively sets up a demand for evidence that goes beyond what paleography can offer, then criticizes the evidence for failing to meet that demand. This approach is not only unreasonable but dismisses the legitimate function of paleography within manuscript studies.

Hixson's inclusion of redaction-critical examples such as Bultmann and Schmithals further illustrates his underlying motivation. He references scholars who accepted an early date for P52 and still postulated later editorial revisions or redactions to John's Gospel. But these speculative theories are grounded in historical-critical ideology—not empirical manuscript data. They represent a methodological bias, not a disqualification of the manuscript's value. Their acceptance of a second-century redaction of John's Gospel despite P52's early presence in Egypt is not proof against early authorship—it merely demonstrates the elasticity of redaction criticism, which often treats textual history as a literary construct rather than a historical transmission.

Hixson rightly states that P52's existence in Egypt by the early to mid-second century does not "prove" Johannine authorship or canonical finality, but no responsible scholar has claimed otherwise. Instead, P52's early date narrows the plausible window for redaction theories and supports the traditional view that the Gospel of John was composed and circulating well before the mid-second century. If P52 is accurately dated to 100–150 C.E., or more conservatively 110–125 C.E., and was found in Egypt, it implies that John's Gospel had not only been authored but also copied and geographically disseminated to a distant region of the Roman Empire—hardly the profile of a late second-century literary product.

Elijah Hixson's Statement:

> "Technically, such a date does not prove that John's Gospel was in its 'final' (canonical) form by then, nor does it prove that the text it contains is any more than a few months old."

Response:

This assertion once again misrepresents the purpose and limitations of paleographic dating. No serious textual scholar has claimed that a paleographically dated manuscript like P52 can prove the final canonical form of a New Testament book. The purpose of dating manuscripts is not to determine canon status or precise textual finality but to establish chronological proximity to the original composition and transmission history.

Moreover, Hixson's suggestion that the fragment may contain a text only "a few months old" borders on speculative rhetoric. He offers no manuscript evidence for such a claim—only a theoretical possibility divorced from transmission realities. The manuscript contains John 18:31–33, 37–38—material that is stylistically and thematically Johannine, with no internal markers suggesting a redacted or transitional form. Scholars have long acknowledged that the text of P52 aligns closely with the Alexandrian tradition, and its conformity to that tradition further undercuts the notion that it represents a radically different or embryonic form of the Gospel.

The mention of "canonical form" also invokes the lens of canonical criticism—another sub-discipline of the historical-critical method—which often casts doubt on the early stability of New Testament texts. But this method begins with skeptical assumptions that stand in contrast to the documentary and historical evidence. From Irenaeus in the late second century to the Muratorian Fragment, there is strong and early external evidence affirming the fourfold Gospel collection, including John, as recognized and authoritative well before the fourth century.

Finally, Hixson's statement subtly implies that unless every feature of the Gospel was finalized, no manuscript can be used to support early authorship. But this kind of absolutism would render most manuscript evidence useless for historical analysis. P52 does not need to prove canonical finality to be valuable. Its value lies in its existence, geographical location (Egypt), and its alignment with the established text of John—all of which support the conclusion that John's Gospel was in circulation by the early second century and thus likely composed in the first.

Elijah Hixson's Statement:

"An early date of P52 might render these possibilities unlikely—even extremely unlikely—but it cannot disprove them."

Response:

Hixson continues with the same strawman strategy—insisting that P52 does not *disprove* theories of a late final redaction of John's Gospel. But again, no textual critic or conservative scholar has ever claimed that paleography *disproves* redactional theories in the absolute. Rather, the argument is cumulative and historical. An early manuscript like P52, dated by many leading paleographers to 100–150 C.E., significantly increases the probability that John's Gospel was already written, copied, and distributed across geographic regions within decades of the apostle's lifetime. This kind of evidence strongly undercuts the plausibility of late redaction dates in the 160s–180s C.E., as proposed by Bultmann or Schmithals.

Further, by stating that such possibilities remain—even if extremely unlikely—Hixson implicitly shifts the standard of proof to one of absolute falsifiability, as though all conservative claims must meet courtroom-level standards of disproof, while speculative critical theories may stand indefinitely if they cannot be utterly refuted. This is not a balanced standard of academic engagement. In historical disciplines, we assess likelihood, coherence with other evidence, and explanatory power. The presence of a Johannine fragment in Egypt from the early second century *greatly diminishes* the plausibility of late redaction theories. It may not disprove them in a mathematical sense, but historical inquiry rarely operates on absolute disproof—it operates on weight of evidence.

To assert that extreme improbabilities should still be left on the table, despite mounting manuscript and patristic evidence to the contrary, reflects a methodological skepticism that becomes unproductive. One could, by similar logic, argue that perhaps the Gospel of John was fabricated entirely in the second century and backdated, or that P52 is a forgery—possibilities that, while technically conceivable, have no evidential basis and deserve no serious place in scholarly discourse. When Hixson says "it cannot disprove them," he opens the door for endless speculative retreats to improbable theories, all while ignoring the textual, geographical, and historical force of P52 as corroborative evidence for early Johannine authorship.

Elijah Hixson's Statement:

"Two examples from redaction-critical commentaries demonstrate this point. First, Rudolf Bultmann accepted a date of P52 in the period of AD 100–150 and still argued that as much as forty years could have passed between the original writing of John's Gospel and a final redaction that left it in the canonical form we have today. Second, Walter Schmithals was well aware of the existence of P52, but he still dated a final redaction of John's Gospel to around AD 160–180."

Response:

Here, Hixson appeals to the opinions of redaction-critical scholars who were unmoved by the implications of P52. But referencing Bultmann and Schmithals—both of whom operated under layers of historical-critical assumptions divorced from the grammatical-historical method—does not strengthen Hixson's point. It simply illustrates that scholars with prior ideological commitments can persist in speculative theories regardless of hard manuscript evidence.

Bultmann, in particular, built his theology around existentialism and was deeply influenced by German idealism, often preferring theological constructs over textual data. His readiness to fragment the Gospel of John into multiple layers of redaction was not driven by manuscript evidence but by presuppositions that the text was too theologically developed to be first-century. Similarly, Schmithals worked from the assumption that significant theological evolution had to occur post-apostolically, thus placing the "final form" of John's Gospel in the late second century.

Citing these scholars does not invalidate the early dating of P52. Rather, it reveals the philosophical precommitments driving much of redaction criticism. Hixson's attempt to reinforce skepticism by pointing to scholars who refused to revise their late-dating models—even in the face of tangible evidence—is not a strength but a weakness. It amounts to an argument that says: "We should remain cautious about early dating because some scholars refused to change their minds despite evidence." That is not a reason to distrust the evidence; it's a demonstration of how bias can override it.

Indeed, if anything, the persistence of Bultmann and Schmithals in the face of P52 demonstrates how doctrinaire the historical-critical method can become when committed to late dating and layered redaction hypotheses. It shows that paleographical evidence like P52 is not being evaluated objectively within those circles but is instead filtered through the grid of higher-critical skepticism. For those using a grammatical-historical method grounded in real manuscript and contextual analysis, the presence of a Johannine fragment dated to 100–150 C.E. in Egypt speaks powerfully to the Gospel's early authorship and circulation.

Elijah Hixson's Statement:

> "Given the uncertain nature of paleographical dating and the fact that P52 has not deterred source-critical scholars from adopting second-century dates of a final redaction to John's Gospel, we quote again Paul Foster's remarks about the usefulness of P52: 'Was John's Gospel written before the end of the first century? Yes, probably.'"

Response:

This statement from Hixson continues the pattern of overstating the limitations of paleography while underplaying the cumulative value of early manuscript evidence. His use of the phrase "uncertain nature of paleographical dating" is accurate in a general sense—scholars recognize that such dating involves ranges, not pinpointed years. However, to emphasize this uncertainty to the degree that it neuters the evidential significance of a manuscript like P52 is disingenuous.

The suggestion that P52 "has not deterred" source-critical scholars from late-dating the final redaction of John's Gospel says more about the rigidity of those scholars than it does about the manuscript itself. If source-critical scholars, operating under speculative and often atheological frameworks, refuse to adjust their theories in light of early evidence, that is an indictment of their method—not the validity of the manuscript.

The quotation from Paul Foster—"Was John's Gospel written before the end of the first century? Yes, probably"—is a half-concession, reflecting the kind of hedged language often used by those unwilling to step too far outside the skeptical academic consensus. Yet this tepid affirmation still supports the traditional and early view, even if Foster couches it with soft qualifiers.

More importantly, the phrase "uncertain nature of paleographical dating" must be understood rightly. Uncertain does not mean "useless" or "without value." It means "approximate within a known range." As stated earlier, paleographical dating operates within terminus post quem (earliest possible) and terminus ante quem (latest possible) parameters. In the case of P52, that range—100–150 C.E.—is conservative and consistent with established practice. Roberts himself said it was "most probably written" during that period, and that phrasing is careful, not presumptive.

Further, it is worth pointing out the irony: scholars like Hixson and Nongbri use paleography to critique paleographic conclusions. They rely on the same discipline to undermine its own earlier judgments without acknowledging that all paleographic assessments—including theirs—operate within the same range-bound uncertainty. Their critique becomes circular: they question the reliability of Roberts's date by using newer but equally uncertain paleographic data, while pretending their own is somehow more definitive or superior.

Ultimately, the real question is not whether P52 proves Johannine authorship by John himself. The fragment, even if it were dated precisely to 125 C.E., cannot answer that directly. What it does show is that John's Gospel was in circulation by that time and had already reached Egypt—a significant geographical distance from its place of origin. That fact alone is weighty and leans heavily in favor of a composition date well within the first century, despite whatever "redaction-critical" speculations are floated by ideologically driven scholars.

Elijah Hixson's Statement:

> "Two examples from redaction-critical commentaries demonstrate this point. First, Rudolf Bultmann accepted a date of P52 in the period of AD 100–150 and still argued that as much as forty years could have passed between the original writing of John's Gospel and a final redaction that left it in the canonical form we have today. Second, Walter Schmithals was well aware of the existence of P52, but he still dated a final redaction of John's Gospel to around AD 160–180."

Response:

This is a classic case of appealing to extreme critical scholarship to undercut the historical reliability of the Gospel of John. Hixson references Bultmann and Schmithals—two scholars who epitomize the height of redaction-critical speculation in the 20th century—not to establish factual data, but to sow doubt about the canonical stability of the Gospel text during the early second century. It's a subtle way of saying: "Even if the manuscript is early, it doesn't mean the Gospel was finalized yet."

Yet this is misleading. Bultmann and Schmithals operated under a radical skepticism that assumed rather than proved late editorial layers to the Gospel of John. These theories are built not on manuscript evidence, but on hypothetical reconstructions of supposed source strata and theological development within the text—none of which has ever been corroborated by textual evidence. In fact, manuscript finds consistently show a high degree of textual stability.

Moreover, citing such scholars sidesteps the actual significance of P52: its textual alignment with later Alexandrian witnesses. Despite its fragmentary nature, the wording of John 18:31–33, 37–38 on P52 matches closely with that of codices like Vaticanus and Sinaiticus. This continuity across time and geography speaks against theories of extensive redaction or late canonical crystallization.

The logic presented by Hixson and the redaction-critical school is circular: they assume that the text was fluid and unstable well into the mid-second century, and therefore interpret early manuscripts through that lens—even when the manuscripts themselves contradict that assumption. This is not historical inquiry; it's dogma disguised as scholarship.

Furthermore, the presence of the Gospel of John in Egypt by the early second century, evidenced by P52, presupposes a period of composition, copying, and transmission sufficient for the text to be circulated beyond its point of origin. If the Gospel was still undergoing major redactional revision in A.D. 160–180, as Schmithals suggests, it could not possibly have appeared in Egypt circa 125 C.E., even in fragmentary form.

Therefore, while Bultmann and Schmithals are part of the scholarly record, they should not be treated as reliable guides on the question of Johannine authorship or textual finality. Their work represents a speculative branch of criticism that imposes modern literary theories onto ancient texts, often with little regard for the actual manuscript evidence. P52, by contrast, is real, tangible, datable, and stable in its textual form. It speaks louder than hypothetical redactional layers ever could.

Elijah Hixson's Statement:

"Given the uncertain nature of paleographical dating and the fact that P52 has not deterred source-critical scholars from adopting second-century dates of a final redaction to John's Gospel, we quote again Paul Foster's remarks about the usefulness of P52: 'Was John's Gospel written before the end of the first century? Yes, probably.'" (p. 104)

Response:

This is yet another attempt to undermine the evidentiary value of P52 through rhetorical hedging and appeal to skepticism. Let's break it down.

First, Hixson invokes the "uncertain nature of paleographical dating" as if this inherent limitation renders the method almost valueless. But this is a misrepresentation. All scholars—including those who advocate for a later date—use paleography to construct relative chronologies. Even those who criticize Roberts' dating of P52 rely on paleography themselves. The issue isn't whether paleography is uncertain; the issue is how much weight one assigns to that uncertainty.

Scholars like C. H. Roberts, T. C. Skeat, Kenyon, and others never claimed paleography could deliver absolute precision. That's why Roberts said we may accept the early second century "with some confidence." He didn't say "with certainty." It is a measured, qualified assessment, not a dogmatic assertion. Hixson's criticism, therefore, attacks a straw man. No one has ever claimed P52 alone absolutely proves Johannine authorship in the first century. But it does provide strong *corroborating* evidence consistent with such a claim.

Second, the appeal to Paul Foster's "Yes, probably" adds nothing substantive to the discussion. It's merely an example of scholarly caution translated into rhetorical ambiguity. Foster's statement is not based on new evidence, nor does it engage with the wealth of internal and external indicators pointing to a first-century origin for John's Gospel. It's a shrug disguised as a conclusion.

Third, the assertion that "P52 has not deterred source-critical scholars from adopting second-century dates of a final redaction" actually undercuts Hixson's argument. The fact that some critics remain unmoved by hard manuscript data says more about their predispositions than it does about the evidence. If P52—an early second-century fragment in close alignment with the Alexandrian tradition—cannot shake their confidence in a late canonical redaction, then no evidence ever will. That's not scholarship; it's ideological entrenchment.

And again, source criticism and redaction criticism are speculative constructs. They posit layers of hypothetical editors and theological communities with little to no manuscript support. P52 is actual, physical, and consistent in form. The burden of proof lies on those who reject what the manuscript evidence plainly suggests: that the Gospel of John, in a recognizably stable form, was copied and circulated by the early second century—likely composed in the late first.

Finally, Hixson's reliance on doubt as a methodological stance reflects a broader trend in modern textual criticism: moving from evidentiary confidence to methodological skepticism. But caution is not the same as cynicism. While no dating method is infallible, the convergence of paleographical comparisons, historical considerations, and textual stability all point toward an early second-century date for P52—and by necessary implication, a first-century date for the composition of the Gospel of John.

Elijah Hixson's Statement:

"A few considerations provide reason for revising Roberts's early date for P52 ('most probably' AD 100–150). First, Roberts's two closest matches to the hand of P52 were not themselves securely dated. Second, the securely dated specimens in general were not close matches. Third, there are now many more published manuscripts with which to compare P52 than when Roberts first published it in 1935, such that consensus regarding the paleographic dates can change. In the case of one of the two 'close matches'—P.Egerton 2—it did. Roberts compared P52 to an early dated manuscript that is no longer considered to be so early. A recent redating of P.Egerton 2 concluded that it dates to circa AD 150–250 and that 'it is not impossible that [P.Egerton 2] was produced sometime at the turn of the third century.'" (Hixson, p. 102)

Response:

Hixson here provides a detailed rationale for reassessing Roberts's dating of P52, based largely on the modern reevaluation of comparison samples and the expansion of available papyrological evidence. However, while this sounds methodologically rigorous on the surface, it is built upon a framework of unrealistic expectations and misapplications of paleographic standards.

Let's address each of the three points in turn.

First, Hixson asserts that Roberts's two closest comparisons were not "securely dated." But what qualifies as "securely dated"? Presumably, Hixson is referring to documentary papyri with internal dates or those linked archaeologically to a fixed time. But literary manuscripts such as P52—indeed, nearly all New Testament papyri—are rarely "securely dated" in this rigid sense. To demand secure dating for literary comparisons imposes a documentary standard on a genre that fundamentally lacks those internal anchors. Roberts's comparisons were literary to literary, which is methodologically appropriate and accepted in the field. This objection thus sets up an impossible standard that no literary manuscript could meet.

Second, Hixson claims that "securely dated specimens in general were not close matches." Again, this reflects the same category error. Paleographers are well aware that documentary and literary hands differ significantly in purpose, execution, and scribal context. As E.G. Turner emphasized, confidence is best when "like is compared with like." That means comparing literary hands to literary hands—not demanding that a Gospel fragment conform to the style of a tax receipt or lease contract. Hixson's criticism assumes a pool of "securely dated" comparanda from the wrong category of writing.

Third, Hixson appeals to the growth of the manuscript corpus and claims that consensus can change with new discoveries. This is valid in principle, and indeed a good reason to remain open to refining dates. But in practice, it has often led not to refinement but to overcorrection. For instance, the redating of P.Egerton 2 was based on weak evidence, mainly the appearance of a hooked apostrophe. This is a minor feature whose chronological significance is far from decisive, as even Turner acknowledged. The claim that P.Egerton 2 could be "sometime at the turn of the third century" is both vague and speculative. It is a hypothesis, not a settled conclusion.

It should also be noted that most major redatings of papyri toward later centuries have not been substantiated by strong, cumulative manuscript parallels. Instead, they are driven by a handful of minor scribal features (such as serifs, ligatures, or spacing conventions) which may vary significantly even within a single century. Such features should not outweigh the overall style and execution of the hand, which is what Roberts, Kenyon, Bell, and others originally used to assign P52 to the early second century.

In sum, Hixson's objections to Roberts's work hinge more on methodological suspicion than on the presence of clearly superior evidence. His appeal to "consensus" subtly masks the fact that the new consensus is built on weak comparisons, cross-genre assumptions, and a scholarly climate increasingly skeptical of early datings in general. If anything, that should caution us not to reject the careful and disciplined work of earlier paleographers too quickly.

Elijah Hixson's Statement:

> "Some scholars who are neither trained papyrologists nor paleographers have proposed unusually early or narrow dates for P52, and these dates should not be accepted. Karl Jaroš (AD 80–125), Philip Comfort (AD 110–125), and Carsten Peter Thiede (AD 80–130) are each controversial for their early dates, which have failed to gain scholarly acceptance." (Hixson, 105)

Response:

This statement by Hixson is a textbook example of the fallacy known as an "appeal to authority," combined with an ad hominem circumstantial fallacy. Instead of engaging the substance of the arguments and evidence presented by these scholars—especially Comfort, who has produced extensive paleographical and textual-critical work—Hixson attempts to dismiss them outright on the basis that they are "not trained papyrologists." This is a non-substantive objection that ignores both the content of their analysis and their actual credentials.

Take Dr. Philip Wesley Comfort as a primary example. His academic qualifications are not in question. He earned two doctorates and studied under the respected textual critic Jacobus H. Petzer. Comfort served as a senior editor for Bible reference materials at Tyndale House Publishers for 25 years and has held academic positions in Greek and New Testament at institutions like Trinity Episcopal Seminary and Wheaton College. He has written over fifteen books on New Testament textual criticism and paleography. Many of these works—published over three decades—are standard reference materials, including detailed transcriptions and paleographic assessments of the earliest New Testament papyri.

Moreover, Comfort has personally examined in detail 25 of the earliest New Testament papyri and has conducted his analysis using both in-person inspection and high-resolution imagery. He is one of the few modern scholars who has taken the time to collate, describe, and date the earliest NT manuscripts with such consistency and transparency. This level of sustained, firsthand engagement with the primary data should merit a fair hearing, not condescension.

To say Comfort's dating "failed to gain scholarly acceptance" is both misleading and selectively framed. It depends entirely on which "scholarly circle" one chooses to emphasize. Many conservative textual scholars, including Dan Wallace and Charles Hill, while perhaps not always agreeing on exact dates, recognize the value and depth of Comfort's manuscript studies. The fact that his early dating challenges the current skeptical consensus is not a reason to dismiss it—it is precisely why it should be evaluated on the merits.

Also, the critique assumes that formal training is the sole gatekeeper to valid paleographic insight. That is demonstrably false. Some of the most influential papyrologists in history—such as Sir Frederic Kenyon and E.G. Turner—were not "formally trained" in the narrow sense that Hixson implies, but developed their authority through rigorous primary research.

Comfort has done the same. His conclusions may be disputed, but not because he is unqualified.

As for Thiede and Jaroš, it is true that their views have not had lasting influence. But again, that is not proof that their arguments were inherently flawed—it only proves that the majority did not adopt them. Scholarly consensus has often erred in the past. Truth is not determined by vote count. What matters is the strength of the evidence, the logic of the argument, and the fidelity to the data.

This type of dismissive rhetoric—labeling dissenters as "unqualified"—functions more as an attempt to manage boundaries within the guild than to advance the discussion. Rather than scrutinize the paleographic reasoning of these men, Hixson simply categorizes them as illegitimate. That is not scholarship; it is gatekeeping.

Dr. Comfort's credibility is not merely academic—it is established through decades of labor-intensive engagement with the actual manuscript evidence. He has devoted more time, effort, and scholarship to the study of the early papyri than any living scholar in the field. His familiarity with both documentary and literary papyri is unmatched in modern textual criticism. From his early work in the 1990s to his extensive cataloging and analysis in *The Text of the Earliest New Testament Greek Manuscripts*, Comfort has contributed a massive body of research that few, if any, contemporary scholars can parallel. While his conclusions have at times stirred debate, it is precisely because of the weight of his documentation and the sheer breadth of his comparative analysis. No one else has done more to make the earliest Greek New Testament papyri accessible, transcribed, translated, and dated for scholarly use. Ignoring his conclusions simply because they run counter to more skeptical views is not responsible scholarship—it is selective and ideological filtering. It is ironic that Hixon, who has only invested a minute fraction of the time and work Comfort has, turns around and levels the very accusation he claims to condemn—dismissing solid scholarship due to perceived theological motivations rather than evaluating the substance of the evidence itself.

Hixson:

> "Of the paleographers who are trained specialists, those who have written most recently have generally argued for a broader date range for P52, including Brent Nongbri (second or even third century), Michael Gronewald (no earlier than ca. AD 200), Don Barker (late second or early third), and Pasquale Orsini and Willy Clarysse (third century)." (Hixson, 105)

Response:

The appeal to "recent" paleographers in contrast to earlier experts like C. H. Roberts, Kenyon, or Deissmann is a chronological fallacy—specifically, the appeal to novelty. The suggestion is that newer opinions must be better simply because they are more recent. This ignores the fact that earlier paleographers were often closer in time to the discovery of comparative papyri, many of which were published and cataloged under their supervision, and they worked with firsthand access to the papyri themselves. Additionally, most of the scholars Hixson names—Nongbri, Gronewald, Barker, Orsini, and Clarysse—rely on comparisons between P52 and either documentary hands or other manuscripts of uncertain or contested dating. Moreover, many of them emphasize ambiguity and uncertainty not on the basis of stronger manuscript parallels, but from a methodological skepticism that leans into Higher Criticism and away from any confidence in textual stability or transmission in early Christianity. These broader date ranges often stem from methodological hesitancy rather than any decisive new paleographic breakthrough.

Furthermore, the tendency among some of these scholars to favor the third century rests on questionable redatings of comparison manuscripts, like the Egerton Gospel, or the elevation of minute features such as hooked apostrophes as determinative, when in reality such features appear in securely dated second-century texts (as shown earlier). Their motivations often appear to be more about pushing back against what they perceive as the apologetic misuse of P52 rather than offering strong positive arguments from paleographic evidence. These modern redaters also seem to commit the very mistake they accuse early scholars of—allowing their theological or ideological commitments to color their interpretation of the evidence. It is difficult to ignore the irony that, in accusing early Christian paleographers of potential apologetic bias, they themselves bring skeptical bias to the table, which leads to unnecessary chronological stretching of the data.

Hixson:

> "Scholars should cite the range of paleographic dates for P52 as broadly as is warranted by the evidence. A range of AD 100–200 is a reasonable window, with AD 125–175 as a slightly narrower possibility. The earlier the date assigned to P52, the more caution scholars should exercise." (Hixson, p. 105)

Response:

This is a veiled attempt to shift the center of gravity away from the original consensus of 100–150 C.E. proposed by C. H. Roberts and supported by a cadre of respected paleographers and textual critics for nearly a century. Hixson's proposal to expand the range to 100–200 C.E., or even 125–175 C.E., is not necessarily based on new or superior paleographic comparisons but rather a methodological unease with the implications of early dating. This trend toward caution often masquerades as academic neutrality, but in practice it serves to erode confidence in early Christian textual transmission without sufficient warrant.

To propose a broader range is not inherently problematic—provided there is solid paleographic evidence to justify it. But when that range is expanded not because of clearly superior manuscript parallels or dated examples but simply to avoid potential theological conclusions (i.e., affirming the Gospel of John's early composition), it becomes ideological caution rather than scholarly rigor. The preference for ambiguity over specificity, especially when the narrower range of 100–150 C.E. has stood the test of time under intense scrutiny, is a symptom of the postmodern influence that has increasingly infected areas of biblical scholarship.

Furthermore, Hixson's statement, "The earlier the date assigned to P52, the more caution scholars should exercise," subtly suggests that early dating is inherently suspect and thus requires a higher burden of proof. This is not a standard applied evenly across paleography. No such cautions are voiced when dates trend later, or when later dates are used to support theories of textual development or redaction. Early dates are treated with suspicion because of what they *imply*—namely, the early existence, transmission, and stability of canonical New Testament texts. But caution should be directed not merely at what date one proposes, but how well that date is supported by direct manuscript comparison, paleographic features, and reasonable inferences. In the case of P52, that remains best represented by the traditional 100–150 C.E. range.

Hixson:

"Of course, as E. G. Turner has said, 'There are too many uncertainties attaching to the paleographical dating of a literary hand for the results to be very significant.' The date of P52 remains uncertain, and it is misleading to present it as if it were not." (Hixson, p. 105)

Response:

Quoting Turner in this context introduces ambiguity by misapplying his cautionary principle. Turner was rightly addressing the inherent limits of paleographic dating—particularly when attempting to pin down exact years. However, Hixson appropriates this statement to imply that paleographic dating, especially in the case of literary hands like P52, is essentially inconsequential. That is not what Turner intended. Turner's point was that paleographic conclusions must be drawn carefully and should rely on comparative data of like with like (literary to literary, formal to formal), not that they are devoid of value or incapable of yielding a reasonable date range.

It is important to remember that Turner, though cautious, was not paralyzed by skepticism. He himself participated in dating manuscripts and relied on paleographic features to do so. To cite Turner as if he were warning against paleography itself misrepresents his balanced stance. Turner's real emphasis was on appropriate methodology and comparative analysis—not on defaulting to indecision or methodological paralysis.

Hixson's use of Turner here also fails to engage with the fact that Turner accepted literary paleography as a viable dating method when carefully applied. If Turner's caution disqualified literary paleography from producing meaningful results, then most of the early dating work of the 20th century—including by Turner himself—would have to be discarded. Yet no one, including Hixson, is prepared to take that step across the board. What we are witnessing is selective skepticism. Paleography is treated as unreliable only when it threatens critical or redactional theories that presuppose late development and canonical instability.

Moreover, stating that "the date of P52 remains uncertain" is itself misleading. Every discipline involving historical inference carries a level of uncertainty. In paleography, *uncertain* does not mean *useless* or *unreliable*. The 100–150 C.E. range proposed by Roberts, and supported by Kenyon, Deissmann, Bell, and others, is not merely a guess—it is a judgment based on methodological comparison with other literary papyri. The supposed uncertainty is not significantly greater than in countless other paleographic assessments accepted as standard in the field. Uncertainty, in this context, is often weaponized to cast doubt, not to clarify.

Hixson:

> "There is nothing unusual or groundbreaking in saying that the date of P52 is uncertain and that paleographic dating is inherently subjective. That has always been the case. The difference is that in the early twentieth century, some biblical scholars emphasized the earliest possible dates of manuscripts (sometimes ignoring the later ends of date ranges) because they believed those dates supported theological convictions. Today, we are more cautious and aware of our presuppositions." (Hixson, p. 105)

Response:

This is an extraordinary statement—not because of its scholarly humility, but because of its subtle sleight of hand. Hixson attempts to frame the entire early 20th-century scholarly consensus surrounding P52's early dating as tainted by theological bias. He contrasts this with what he claims is a new age of cautious, self-aware scholarship, which, apparently, has risen above such partiality. However, this revisionist framing unjustly dismisses the rigor of early paleographers like C. H. Roberts, Frederic Kenyon, Adolf Deissmann, and W. H. P. Hatch—men who applied careful comparative analysis and worked with the best available parallels, many of which are still considered valid today.

To accuse these foundational scholars of overemphasizing early dates due to theological presuppositions without offering documented evidence is to commit the fallacy of poisoning the well. It smuggles in an ad hominem attack under the guise of caution. Moreover, it fails to apply the same standard of scrutiny to modern redaters like Brent Nongbri, Don Barker, or Hixson himself. Are we to believe they operate in a vacuum, unaffected by their own scholarly presuppositions, institutional pressures, or ideological leanings? The assertion that today's scholars are more "aware of our presuppositions" ironically overlooks the fact that this supposed awareness does not automatically translate into objectivity or neutrality. Skepticism and hyper-caution can be just as biased as premature certainty.

Further, Hixson's comment subtly shifts the goalposts. Instead of arguing on the basis of paleographic features or textual parallels, he introduces sociological speculation—implying that past scholars were motivated by confessional agendas. But again, we must ask: what about the motivations of those who wish to delay the dating of P52? Are they not also influenced by the implications of their conclusions? A second-century P52 threatens modern critical theories that assign late redaction to the Gospel of John. Redating it into the third century thus becomes a theological safeguard for liberal redaction criticism.

Finally, Hixson's implication that we are merely repeating an early-century error is misleading. As shown, many paleographers of today—such as Philip Comfort, David Barrett, and even the Alands—have reaffirmed the early second-century date based on sound comparative analysis, not dogma. It is not a theological stance to believe that P52 may date from 100–125 C.E.; it is a paleographic judgment supported by the evidence and by scholars who have invested entire careers in analyzing ancient Greek scripts.

Hixson:

"Fourth, some Christian apologists have also overstated what P52 can prove. For example, Josh McDowell claims, 'The dating of the Rylands Papyrus has great significance. It proves the Gospel of John was being copied and disseminated within the lifetime of some of John's contemporaries and eyewitnesses of Christ.' But this simply cannot be proven from the dating of P52, no matter how early the manuscript may be." (Hixson, p. 105)

Response:

Here again we observe Hixson's recurring tactic—redirecting the academic discussion of manuscript dating into a critique of apologetic overreach. While it is important to clarify what manuscripts can and cannot prove, Hixson's statement gives the impression that any theological or apologetic implication drawn from an early dating is inherently illegitimate. This is a false dichotomy. There is a vast difference between saying P52 *proves* eyewitness authorship and saying that P52 strongly *supports* or is *consistent with* such a conclusion.

Josh McDowell's statement, while perhaps enthusiastic, is not without merit when taken in historical context. If P52 is dated to 100–125 C.E., that would place its production within just a few decades of the traditional date for the Gospel of John (c. 85–90 C.E.), and potentially within the lifespans of those who knew John personally. This does not "prove" eyewitness testimony, but it certainly strengthens the case, especially when paired with the consistent internal and external evidence affirming Johannine authorship.

Hixson, however, uses this as an opportunity to push back not against McDowell's particular wording, but against any confident implication drawn from early manuscript evidence. This pattern reflects a broader disposition among some modern scholars who resist apologetic conclusions not because the evidence contradicts them, but because such conclusions are seen as theologically motivated and therefore suspect. But textual scholarship must be driven by the evidence itself—not by fear of who might cite it or how it might be used.

Moreover, we could just as easily reverse the concern. Is Hixson's own reaction not also an overstatement in the other direction? If P52 cannot *prove* that John's Gospel was already in wide circulation by 125 C.E., neither can a skeptical attitude *disprove* it. And yet Hixson's language often functions rhetorically to give that impression. The proper approach is not to downplay the significance of P52 but to interpret it within a broader evidential framework, which includes the manuscript's provenance, the reliability of early patristic citations, and the consensus of early church tradition.

THE P52 PROJECT

There is nothing methodologically unsound in using P52 as a meaningful data point to support traditional authorship and early dissemination—especially when the document was found in Egypt, far from Ephesus, where John likely wrote. Such a geographic spread of the Gospel of John implies an even earlier date for its composition and transmission. Again, Hixson's critique does not so much refute McDowell's conclusion as it reveals a discomfort with the theological implications of the manuscript evidence.

Hixson:

"Finally, it is unfortunate that some otherwise trustworthy Christian apologists have made such claims based on outdated information. For example, Craig Evans wrote, 'What this means is that the Gospel of John was written before 100 C.E., quite possibly before 90 C.E.' when P52 was first published, the editors dated it to ca. AD 125. More recent study places it in the later second century." (Hixson, p. 105)

Response:

This criticism presents a misleading narrative. The suggestion that earlier datings are "outdated" is only credible if the newer datings are demonstrably superior—yet this is precisely what remains in contention. Hixson refers to "more recent study" as if the passage of time automatically confers greater accuracy. But paleography is not linear in its advancement; newer is not always better. What matters is the methodology and the comparative evidence—something earlier paleographers like C.H. Roberts, Harold Bell, and W. Schubart grounded in rigorous analysis of stylistic parallels with known manuscripts.

Moreover, to refer to the early dating of P52 (100–150 C.E.) as "outdated" presupposes that there has been a consensus shift among specialists—which is not the case. While a few modern scholars, such as Brent Nongbri, Don Barker, and Michael Gronewald, argue for a later date, many prominent paleographers, including Philip Comfort, David Barrett, and even Kurt and Barbara Aland, maintain that P52 belongs within the earlier second century. The support for this range remains substantial among those with decades of hands-on experience in both literary and documentary Greek papyri. In fact, many so-called "recent studies" lean on theoretical concerns rather than any decisive paleographical disproof of earlier datings.

The quote from Craig Evans does not present a certainty but a plausible deduction: if P52 can be confidently dated to 100–125 C.E. and was discovered in Egypt, then John's Gospel must have been written, copied, and disseminated prior to that. Even a slightly later date for P52, such as 150 C.E., still supports a first-century origin of the Gospel. The "updated information" that Hixson appeals to is hardly the consensus and, in many cases, relies on circular reasoning: manuscripts are redated based on changes in assumptions about others, which are then used to redated the former.

Additionally, Hixson's final statement subtly reframes the debate. Instead of engaging directly with the paleographical arguments and evidence for an earlier date, he casts doubt on the motives or reliability of Christian apologists like Evans. But this is not a matter of outdated information—it is a matter of competing interpretations. Labeling traditional dates as "outdated" prematurely ends the discussion without demonstrating that the newer dates are objectively superior. It dismisses the arguments by fiat rather than engaging them on their merits.

The underlying problem is not that apologists like Evans are behind the times, but that scholars like Hixson dismiss as obsolete any viewpoint that does not align with a more skeptical or minimalistic timeline. In doing so, they assume the very conclusions they should be trying to prove. Paleography is a field grounded in careful analysis, not revisionist trends, and no amount of academic fashion can erase the fact that a substantial number of credentialed scholars—many with greater experience in paleographic comparison than Hixson—still affirm the traditional dating of P52 to the first half of the second century.

Hixson:

"Again, the date of a manuscript does not prove the date of the text it contains. The most that can be said about the date of P52 is that some form of the Gospel of John existed in Egypt in the second century." (Hixson, p. 105)

Response:

This statement exemplifies a common yet misleadingly reductionist approach. Of course, manuscript evidence does not *prove* authorship or the exact date of original composition with mathematical certainty. But it does serve as critical *evidence*—evidence that, when combined with historical, textual, and transmission data, supports strong conclusions. No one claims that P52, on its own, definitively proves that the Gospel of John was written in the first century. That's a strawman. However, its significance lies in what it *does* make possible: the Gospel must have been written, copied, and circulated to Egypt by the early second century, likely decades earlier. That fact alone undercuts the entire framework of those who wish to push the composition or redaction of John's Gospel into the mid-to-late second century.

THE P52 PROJECT

Hixson's phrasing—"some form of the Gospel of John existed in Egypt"—is intentionally vague, perhaps to create the impression that P52 may represent an unstable or fluid textual tradition. Yet the actual content of P52 (John 18:31–33, 37–38) aligns remarkably well with the Alexandrian text-type and shows no signs of radical textual alteration. The fragment testifies to the high level of stability and early dissemination of the Johannine Gospel. The phrase "some form" misleadingly suggests substantial variance, when in fact, we see textual continuity that supports the broader manuscript tradition.

Furthermore, Hixson's formulation downplays the significance of P52's provenance—namely, its discovery in Egypt. For a manuscript fragment of John to be found that far from its likely point of origin (Asia Minor or possibly Ephesus), it presupposes a copying and transmission process that takes time. It had to be copied, disseminated, and transported, possibly through various communities, before it ever arrived in Egypt. This would reasonably place the Gospel's original composition decades earlier, strongly affirming a first-century date.

The conservative view does not rest on a single papyrus fragment but on the cumulative evidence: the internal claims of the Gospel of John (e.g., 21:24), early patristic testimony (e.g., Irenaeus affirming Johannine authorship), manuscript evidence like P52, and the circulation patterns of early Christianity. P52 is one piece in this larger puzzle—but it is a critical piece, and dismissing it as merely showing that "some form" of the text existed in Egypt in the second century is both evasive and reductionist. It amounts to downplaying data that doesn't fit a skeptical agenda.

Hixson:

> "Other scholars, such as Brent Nongbri, have argued that the handwriting of P52 can only be said to look 'early' in a very general sense. Nongbri is a trained papyrologist and his doctoral dissertation focused on the development of Greek book hands in the second and third centuries. He argues that P52 should be dated to the later second or even early third century, and he has offered comparisons with other papyri to support this view." (Hixson, *Myths and Mistakes*, p. 105)

Response:

While Brent Nongbri is a trained papyrologist, his reputation is defined not by objective analysis but by a methodologically skeptical approach that seeks to undermine earlier scholarly consensus without providing more compelling comparative data. His dismissal of P52 as merely "early in a very general sense" is an example of excessive caution bordering on obfuscation. The irony lies in Nongbri's reliance on the very paleographical methods he attempts to undermine. He cites comparable hands—yet these are rarely, if ever, truly parallel to P52 in style or form across the full manuscript. When evaluating papyri, the standard has always been that comparison should involve multiple letters, word spacing, line height, and scribal tendencies—not merely a few shared character shapes.

Moreover, Nongbri's analysis has failed to overturn the considered consensus of C.H. Roberts, T.C. Skeat, and others who evaluated P52 not in isolation but within the wider tradition of early Christian codices, dating it to 100–150 C.E. His redating efforts often hinge on postmodern inclinations to question authority and blur boundaries of evidence. Yet his proposed comparisons, such as P.Oxy. 4803 and P.Bas. 2.43, fall short in matching the overall literary form and execution seen in P52. Furthermore, even Nongbri's own cited comparators (like P. Flor. 1.1) do not demand a redating; rather, they represent a conservative choice to shift dating boundaries without conclusive data. In this context, his view reflects less a robust revision of evidence and more a methodological skepticism that resists any strong claim, even when warranted.

By contrast, Comfort and earlier scholars examined a much broader spectrum of paleographic indicators, cross-referenced manuscript styles, and accounted for the transition from scroll to codex. Their early dating is not dogma—it is an evidence-based judgment shared by many scholars with extensive manuscript experience. Hixson's appeal to Nongbri as an authority fails to show that Nongbri's comparisons are more compelling than those used by Roberts, Kenyon, or Comfort—men who actually spent decades developing typologies and examining thousands of papyri.

Hixson:

"What P52 does show, then, is that John 18 was being read in Egypt in the first half of the second century or later. It offers no support to the notion that John's Gospel must have been written before AD 100, though it is consistent with that idea. A date for John's Gospel in the first century is consistent with P52. That is all we can say, and that is all we need to say. P52 offers no help in evaluating the eyewitness status of John's Gospel." (Hixson, *Myths and Mistakes*, p. 105)

Response:

This concluding summary from Hixson once again reveals his overarching concern: to minimize the evidential value of P52, especially with respect to the dating and authorship of the Gospel of John. While it is technically true that no single manuscript can prove authorship or final canonical form, Hixson's conclusion underrepresents the cumulative force of the manuscript evidence when combined with external patristic testimony and internal literary consistency. What Hixson does not engage with is the chain of probability. If P52 is reasonably dated to the first half of the second century, and it contains a segment of John's Gospel already circulating in Egypt, then logically, the composition of the Gospel itself must predate the copy—by decades, not months. In the ancient world, the transmission of a literary work across geographic boundaries was not instantaneous; it involved copying, transporting, and acceptance within the community.

Hixson insists, "That is all we can say, and that is all we need to say," which smacks more of rhetorical closure than open scholarly analysis. P52 certainly does not "prove" that John was an eyewitness, but when viewed in light of the early second-century patristic writings—such as the references to John's Gospel by Ignatius of Antioch and Polycarp of Smyrna—it strongly supports a first-century origin. What's more, its textual alignment with later Alexandrian manuscripts suggests remarkable textual stability. The idea that John 18 existed in a "pre-canonical" form is speculative and unprovable, driven more by redaction-critical ideology than manuscript evidence.

In conclusion, while Hixson rightly urges scholarly caution, he overcorrects by collapsing legitimate evidentiary value into an excessive minimalism. The conservative position remains: P52, even in its fragmentary state, offers strong external support for a Gospel of John written in the late first century by the apostle John himself, and in canonical form substantially as we have it today. Its presence in Egypt by 125–150 C.E. is not a trivial detail—it is a powerful historical data point in favor of early composition and wide dissemination.

Despite the chorus of skepticism from some modern scholars, the early paleographic dating of P52 remains a defensible position grounded in careful comparative analysis and supported by multiple world-class paleographers. While no manuscript alone proves Johannine authorship or canonical finality, the convergence of early manuscript evidence, internal literary cohesion, and external patristic references offers a compelling picture: John's Gospel was authored by the apostle John in the late first century and was circulating in Egypt by the early to mid-second century. Those who seek to minimize P52's significance often do so not because of the evidence itself but because of presuppositions rooted in historical-critical skepticism. The attempt to dilute the manuscript's value by drawing attention to its fragmentary state, or by leveraging ambiguity to cloud clarity, cannot erase the fact that P52 is one of the strongest early witnesses we possess to the Gospel of John. Conservative scholarship need not retreat in the face of vague objections or academic trendiness. When one follows the evidence where it leads—without the imposition of unnecessary doubt—P52 stands as an early, reliable, and valuable testament to the stability and early circulation of John's Gospel.

Edward D. Andrews

CHAPTER 10 Using Comparative Paleography to Date P52

Philip Comfort writes, "The primary means of dating a New Testament manuscript, as an undated literary text [e.g., P52], is by doing a comparative analysis with the handwriting of other dated documentary texts. The second method is to do a comparative analysis with literary manuscripts having a date based on the association with a documentary text on the recto or verso." Comfort goes on to explain, "As paleographers seek to assign a date to a manuscript, they employ comparative morphology, which is a comparative study of letter forms. Paleographers in the past (such as Kenyon) used to look for a match of certain individual letter forms. This practice called the "test-letter" theory is no longer fully endorsed. Rather, paleographers look at the letters in relation to the entire piece of writing; in other words, it is the overall likeness that constitutes a morphological match. Of course, this doesn't exclude matching letters, but the match must be more than just in a few letters." We have chosen 14 different letters that are the most visible in P52 (alpha, delta, epsilon, eta, iota, kappa, lambda, nu, omicron, pi, sigma, tau, upsilon, and omega). Guglielmo Cavallo, in chapter 5: Greek and Latin Writing in the Papyri, "Palaeographical evidence can emerge from the comparison of dated or datable documentary writing and undated literary hands. In the absence of any other criterion for dating, only a palaeographical assessment remains." He goes on to say, "The skilled hands found in literary papyri of the second and third centuries [C.E.] display a great variety of graphic solutions." He adds, "At this time, the most notable phenomenon in writing found in the domain of skilled and calligraphic hands is the development of normative scripts (i.e., handwritings that follow precise rules and are repetitively stable in their technique and manner of execution, with the result that they have great staying power)."

Style of Writing

The writing styles under consideration for the papyri between 75 – 225 C.E. had many general characteristics. The styles include the Roman Uncial, the Biblical Uncial or Biblical Majuscule, the Decorated Rounded Uncial, and the Severe Style. A style of writing began (came into being, starting point), emerged (apparent), fully developed (all characteristics in play), became prominent (common, well-known), and then faded (gradually disappear). Therefore, it was common for one style to begin and emerge while another was still in play or fading. In fact, the emergence and development of the new style are likely what caused the current style to begin to fade. The time period for the full process from a style beginning (coming into being) to fading (diminishing gradually) can be quite long, but it can also vary.

The appearance of one character being separate or several characters being separate from the others and then the next letter or letters linked by ligatures. What seems to be ligatures in P52 are simply letters touching or bumping into one another.

- There was a roundness and smoothness in the forms of the letters.
- There was a darkening of the characters by going over them again.
- There are decorative serifs in several letters. A serif is a slight projection finishing off a stroke of a letter in certain typefaces.
- The Biblical Uncial has little or no decoration and intentionally alternates between thick and thin strokes of the pen unlike its predecessor, the Roman Uncial.
- An undecorated script began (came into being, starting point) and emerged (apparent) in the late first century, and was fully developed (all characteristics in play) at the beginning of and into the middle of the second century and became prominent (common, well-known) toward the end of the second century C.E. Here we find the character squarer, with a heavy look. The letters are uniform size (except iota, rho, phi, psi, omega), stand upright, and thick and thin strokes are certainly notable.
- There were times when convenience rather than beauty was the primary consideration.
- There was a contrast between thin horizontal strokes and heavier (thicker) vertical ones. (See gamma, pi, tau), with slanted strokes coming in between
- Then, there are the slanted strokes in between (alpha, delta, lambda).
- The Rho and upsilon extend below the baseline.
- The hastas of phi (Φ) and psi (Ψ) extend both up and down.
- All the letters except gamma, rho, phi, psi extend the same level vertically.
- In time, there were no ligatures (connecting letters).
- There was no embellishment at the end of strokes, such as serifs and blobs.

In the following pages, we will use comparative paleography, looking at the various documentary and literary manuscripts dating from about 75–225 C.E. that have been used in the dating and redating of P52. There is no other method for dating an undated literary document as Nongbri and others well know. All parties know that dating a literary by comparing it to other literary texts involves some subjectivity. It is both an art and a science. THE SCIENCE: The one doing the comparing must use the common sense that God gave him or her, being reasonable and rational, avoiding unrealistic expectations, which are unhelpful expectations. We have now heaped doubt on the Christian community when we set aside reasonable, rational, acceptable expectations with unrealistic, unreasonable, irrational expectations. THE SCIENCE: Of course, there are some basic rules and principles in the comparison process. The primary principle would be to look at many different letters in the documents being compared instead of just a few. A second principle would be to identify general similarities instead of some letter form fingerprint that would be an exact match if laid over each other. Another thing to be mindful of is that these different styles of writing did not just show up on the scene and then disappear without a trace. However, there was a time when a style was fully developed (all characteristics in play), became prominent (common, well-known).

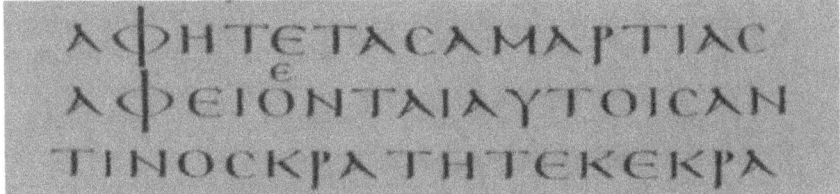

Image Professional Scribe Codex Vaticanus On Parchment

Image Practiced Scribe P52 on Papyrus

Dating would be somewhat easier if the P52 scribe were a professional scribe bookhand instead of a practiced scribe because we would have higher expectations for him. He does seem to try to be consistent, or he is consistent to a degree in the way he writes. He has no intention; it seems to be perfect. But he seems to be trying to do a good job. Some of his letters are more consistent than others. Some you cannot really judge because of the one that looks like a ligature but really is just two or three letters touching, while the others are clearly a stand-alone or at least not being bumped into. He was employing great care in his writing, attention to detail, a kind of unofficial style.

Roberts' observed that "the scribe [of P52] writes in a heavy, rounded and rather elaborate hand, often uses several strokes to form a single letter (cf. the eta and particularly the sigma in Recto, 1. 3) with a rather clumsy effect and is fond of adding a small flourish or hook to the end of his strokes (cf. the omega, the iota and the upsilon); among particular letters the epsilon with its cross stroke a little above the centre, the delta, the upsilon and the mu may be noted. Some of these features can be paralleled from dated documents," as well as literary documents. Roberts adds, "The writer of P. Ryl. Gk. 457 [P52] (as far as one can judge from the scanty evidence) used neither stops nor breathings; his orthography, apart from a couple of itacisms, is good, and his writing, if not that of a practiced scribe, is painstaking and regular. In this respect, the verdict of the editors of P. Egerton 2 upon the writer of that text is applicable to ours: P. Ryl. Gk. 457 also has a somewhat 'informal air' about it and with no claims to fine writing is yet a careful piece of work." Did Roberts' position on P52 change over time? It has been argued that he was young and inexperienced in 1935, a mere 26-years old.

At 68 years old and at the close of an illustrious career in the field of textual studies, paleography, papyrology, he had authored five books, which included, Two Biblical Papyri in the John Rylands Library (1936), The Antinoopolis Papyri (1950), Birth of the Codex (1954), Oxford Palaeographical Handbooks (1955), and Manuscript, Society and Belief in Early Christian Egypt (1977). In the latter, Roberts surveyed fourteen papyri. He believed them to be of Christian origin. Twelve of these were codices, and the other two were scrolls. In 1977, these were all the manuscripts that were commonly viewed as dating to the second century C.E., including P52. Only three of the fourteen he viewed as possessing a handwriting style known as a professional bookhand, that is a professional who was very capable of producing literary works. The other eleven, which included P52, Roberts stated that their scribes were,

> ...not trained in calligraphy and so not accustomed to writing books, though they were familiar with them; they employ what is basically a documentary hand but at the same time they are aware that it is a book and not a document on which they are engaged. They are not personal or private hands; and in most a degree of regularity and of clarity is aimed at and achieved. Such hands may be described as "reformed documentary." (One advantage for the paleographer in such hands is that with their close links to the documents they are somewhat less difficult to date than purely calligraphic hands).

NOTE: This documentary hand that Roberts speaks of sounds more like the reformed documentary hand. As defined today, the reformed documentary hand is a step above the documentary hand as far as the skill of copying a document is concerned. Paleographers have been able to distinguish four major kinds of handwriting, each of which reveals something about the training (or lack thereof) of the copyist who produced it. The four types are as follows:

1.) Common: The work of a semiliterate writer who is untrained in making documents. This handwriting usually displays an inelegant cursive.

2.) Documentary: The work of a literate writer who has had experience in preparing documents. This has also been called "chancery handwriting" (prominent in the period A.D. 200–225). Official scribes used it in public administration.

3.) Reformed documentary: The work of a literate writer who had experience in preparing documents and in copying works of literature. Often, this hand attempts to imitate the work of a professional but does not fully achieve the professional look.

4.) Professional: The work of a professional scribe. These writings display the craftsmanship of what is commonly called a "book hand" or "literary hand" and leave telltale marks of professionalism such as stichoi markings (the tallying of the number of lines, according to which a professional scribe would be paid), as are found in P46.

Various handwriting styles are more pronounced in one time period over another and thereby help in dating manuscripts.

It should be noted that the codex of P52 was done on a good quality papyrus. It had wide margins, it had letters that were clear and generally upright, possessed short lines, decorative script hooks and finials (a decorative feature at the foot of the letter), as well as its bilinear writing (letters being kept with an imaginary upper and lower line, except the alpha, upsilon, iota, and the rho). All of this gives an overall appearance of a copyist who not being of the professional bookhand caliber, he is also not far removed. His letterforms are not as fine as P64 or P77, he is closer to the reformed documentary hand. The scribe that penned P52 knew that he was not working on some legal document but rather a literary work. P52, like many of the other early Greek New Testament papyri, were written in this reformed documentary hand. (P1, P30, P32, P35, P38, P45, P52, P69, P87, P90, P100, P102, P108, P109, P110) When Roberts authors his next book, he is now 74 years old, and it is now 1983, so he is long removed from 1935, and there is absolutely no indication he ever changed his position on the dating of P52 up until the time of his death in 1990.

In The Birth of the Codex, Roberts and Skeat wrote:

THE P52 PROJECT

The Christian manuscripts of the second century, although not reaching a high standard of calligraphy, generally exhibit a competent style of writing which has been called "reformed documentary" and which is likely to be the work of experienced scribes, whether Christian or not.... And it is therefore a reasonable assumption that the scribes of the Christian texts received pay for their work.

Handwriting comparison is not like DNA comparison and fingerprint comparison. With DNA and fingerprints, we will get an exact, absolute match. Handwriting analysis (comparing) is general in its very nature. We are looking for a general pattern, not that every single letter and style or form must match explicitly in every detail with each other.

The idea that "paleography is not the most effective method" or 'using a undated manuscript to date an undated manuscript is circularity of argument' "for dating texts" seems to suggest that a better method is available to us for P52 or all other undated literary manuscripts. That is not the situation, as even Nongbri admits. As I mentioned before, he uses paleography in an effort to undermine P52.

Characteristics

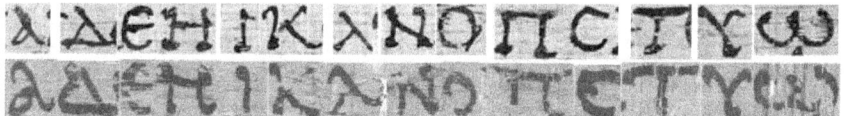

Image P52 (100-150 C.E.) P. 6845 Homer (75-125 C.E.)

On P. 6845, Nongbri agrees but disagrees. He writes, "P.Berol. 6845, to which the original editor assigned a date (on paléographie evidence) in the early second century. There are some definite similarities between letters in the two manuscripts, particularly upsilon and mu, but the pi and alpha of P52 are quite distinct from those of P.Berol. 6845. The epsilon of P.Berol. 6845, with its middle bar consistently approaching and frequently meeting the upper bar, is also different from that of P52. The rho of P.Berol. 6845 does not stretch below the other letters, as does the rho of P52. Overall, the hand is not dissimilar from P52, but, as we shall see, the similarities seen here persist in documents of the third century C.E." (bold mine)

It seems, when someone uses the phrase "not dissimilar" they are trying to downplay the similarity by using the adverb "not" to give the opposite impression mentally of what is true, i.e., there is a definite similarity. Nongbri openly says that there are "some definite similarities." He then gives upsilon and mu as those similarities. He then says, "the pi and alpha of P52 are quite distinct," to which I would disagree about the pi, as you can see in the image above. Moreover, between P52 and P.Berol. 6845, there is definite similarity also between kappa, lambda, nu, upsilon, and omega, as can be seen from the above image.

Image P52 (100-150 C.E.) P. Egerton 2 (150 C.E.)

Clearly, there is much similarity between P52 and P. Egerton 2. Since there has been a redating of P. Egerton 2 to about 200 C.E., a redating that should not be, we will suggest that you read CHAPTER 1 P. Egerton 2.

Image P52 (100-150 C.E.) P.Fayûm 110 (94 C.E.)

Image P.Fayûm 110 end of lines 7-9

On P.Fayûm 110 we find Nongbri still agreeing and disagreeing. He writes, "While Roberts notes that the similarities are not as close, he does provide some parallels from dated documentary papyri. Roberts especially emphasizes the importance of P.Fayûm 110 because it 'shows, as does our text, the simultaneous use of two forms of alpha.' In figure 5, I have enlarged the ends of lines 7-9, which display this characteristic. The alpha of βαθος in line 8 is looped; the alpha of ελαι- at the end of line 7 is not looped, but neither is it arched like the non-looping alpha of P52. The alpha of P.Fayûm

THE P52 PROJECT

110 looks more like the alpha of μαρτυ[ρησω] in line 2 on the verso of P52. The delta is also similar to that of P52."

It seems as though we will have to repeat the development of the manuscript font style and characteristics here as well. A style of writing began (came into being, starting point), emerged (apparent), fully developed (all characteristics in play), became prominent (common, well-known), and then faded (gradually disappear). Therefore, it was common for one style to begin and emerge while another was still in play or fading. In fact, the emergence and development of the new style are likely what caused the current style to begin to fade. The time period for the full process from a style beginning (coming into being) to fading (diminishing gradually) can be quite long, but it can also vary.

The manuscripts that are used to support the early dating of P52 to about 100–150 C.E. have multiple matching letters, not a single matching letter. The phrase that we need to keep in mind is, generally speaking, not absolute certainty. The match of letterforms, generally speaking, is what we look for. Do the forms of the letters look similar in style in P52 itself (alpha, delta, epsilon, eta, iota, kappa, lambda, nu, omicron, pi, sigma, tau, upsilon, and omega)? Largely, when in all the places I see sigma, tau, upsilon, etc., are they similar in form? If the answer is yes, which it is for P52; then, we move on to the documents that have been presented by Roberts and other paleographers and papyrologists since. Is there a general match, not some fingerprint-DNA match? And, once again, the answer is yes. The scribal tendencies of these matching letterforms in P52 and these other dated and undated documents also appear in the center of the fully developed (all characteristics in play) and became prominent (common, well-known) timeline. It seems Nongbri is attempting to find a couple of letterforms at later dates (maybe the fading, diminishing part of the timeline) that have similar features to letters in P52 so as to date P52 to a wider and later date range, i.e., 100-225 C.E.

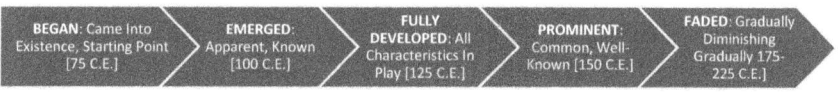

Image The timeline above is simply a visual example and does not necessarily apply to and specific writing style.

Nongbri admits, "I have not radically revised Roberts's work. I have not provided any third-century documentary papyri that are absolute "dead ringers" for the handwriting of P52, and even if I had done so, that would not force us to date P52 at some exact point in the third century." What is Nongbri's worry, then? He states it plainly, "The real problem is thus in the way scholars of the New Testament have used and abused papyrological evidence." What does that mean? For Nongbri and other paleographers and papyrologists, it is troublesome when textual scholars and Christian apologists take the dating of 100-150 C.E. and say that P52 dates more specifically to 100 C.E. or 110 C.E. or even 100-125 C..E. For Nongbri and company that is using and abusing papyrological evidence. But I turn the table on Nongbri and company, in that I find a lot of the newer textual scholars, paleographers, and papyrologists who use and abuse the later dating by referring to 200 C.E. My second point would be, how can a New Testament scholar abuse the evidence of 100-150 C.E. when the date range is 100–150 C.E. if they select and date therein? The papyrologist is telling us any date in between those two ranges is possible. Yes, the New Testament scholar should share the whole range and then if he chooses to highlight an earlier focus, qualify it like, 'so it could date as early as _____.' Also, Nongbri and others see fifty years as too small of a time period for a writing style. They feel that a century or even two centuries is a more suitable range for a writing style.

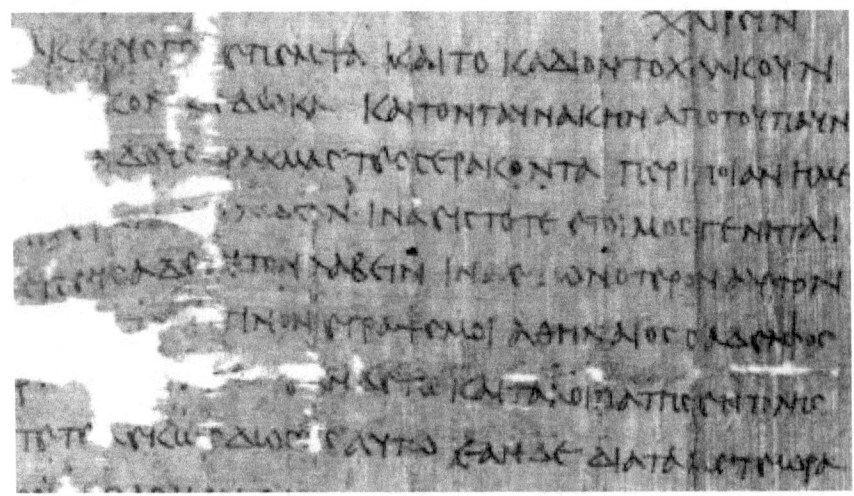

Image P.Lond. 2078_Dated early second century C.E.

Nongbri writes, "He [Roberts] next notes similarities with P.Lond. inv. 2078 (=SB 5.7987), a letter written under the reign of Domitian (81-96 C.E.).36 SB 5.7987, reproduced in figure 6, is, in my opinion, the least convincing of Roberts's parallels. Its upsilon is distinctly different, the alpha has neither arches nor loops and the delta is not at all similar. Only the mu closely resembles that of P52 (and occasionally the rho, as in καισαρος in the middle of the penultimate line)."

Again, I would simply reply that unless we are matching up two very professional scribes, like the one who worked on Codex Vaticanus, we are not to expect some fingerprint-DNA match. Thus, generally speaking, the letters will be similar. Moreover, not every document will be as closely matched like the other. If you are comparing ten manuscripts, one of them has to be the closest or best-matched document, and one of them will have to be the least close matched of the ten, but this does not negate its support. Nongbri says that is "the least convincing of Roberts's parallels." Well, one of them has to be.

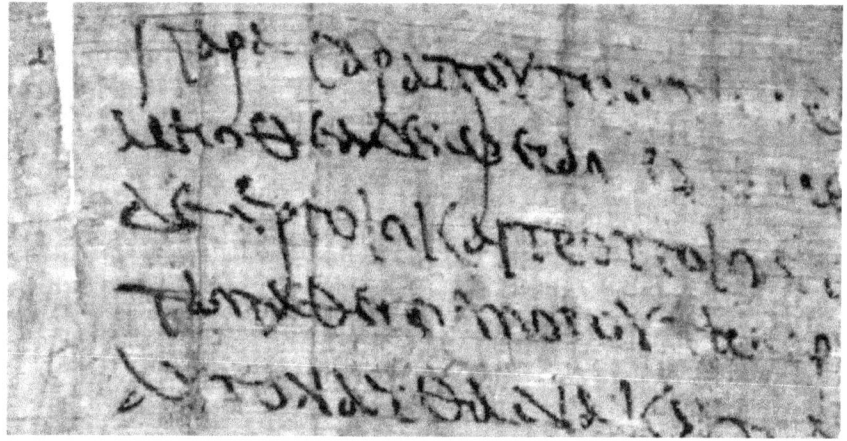

Image P. Oslo 22 (A.D. 127)

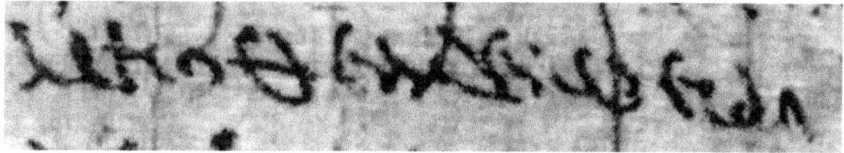

Roberts then refers to "P.Oslo 2.22, here figure 7, a petition to a strategus written in 127 C.E. He sees resemblances in the eta, mu, and iota. In figure 8,1 have enlarged the beginning of line 3, which reads – μης θεαδελφειας and shows all three of those letters. The overall appearance is not terribly close to that of P52, but the letters that Roberts identifies are similar. Some letters, however, are very different, such as the sigma, which curves sharply downward in P.Oslo. 2.22."

Nongbri says, "the overall appearance is not terribly close to that of P52, but the letters that Roberts identifies are similar." Again, we are not looking for an absolute perfect match. Are there several letters that do match? Yes. Nongbri goes on to point out differences once again "Some letters, however, are very different, such as the sigma, which curves sharply downward in P.Oslo. 2.22." Yes, well, this is expected because the scribe of P52 is not a professional scribe; he is a practiced scribe, a reformed documentary hand, which is a literate writer with experience in making copies of literature. There are times when the forms of the letters in P52 does not even match the forms of the letters in P52.

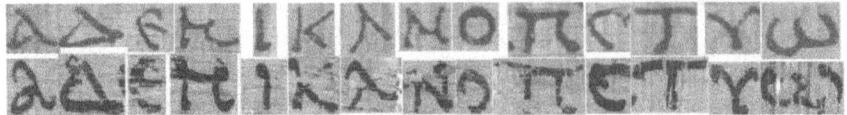

Image (B.G.U. 1.22) P_06854_R_001 [top] and P52 [bottom] dated to 114 C.E. Retrieved from http://berlpap.smb.museum/record/ Tuesday, May 19, 2020

On this Nongbri writes, "The next papyrus Roberts mentions is now known as B.G.U. 1.22 (fig. 9), a document dated to 114 C.E. Roberts does not point out any specific characteristics of this papyrus, and I am uncertain what similarities he sees here. The alpha is different, lacking both the arch and loop of P52's two types of alpha. The vertical stroke of the tau of B.G.U. 1.22 often leans to the right. The upsilon is perhaps similar, but on the whole, this document is not an overly impressive parallel."

Nongbri simply gives you an image of B.G.U. 1.22 alone, while I have given you letters in the above image B.G.U. 1.22 on top of P52. We can see some slight similarities with the alpha, eta, and Tau when we do it this way. But I believe that we have a more significant similarity with the epsilon, the kappa, Nu, and Pi. And an even more likeness with the Upsilon and Omega. Again, we are not comparing two professional scribes here, so the subtle difference is to be expected. It might not be overly impressive, but it isn't unimpressive or mediocre either. We are not expecting some fingerprint-DNA match. Thus, generally speaking, the letters are similar, some more so than others. Again, not every document will be as closely matched as the other.

THE P52 PROJECT

Image P.Mich. inv. 5336 (=SB 22.15782). A petition dated to 152 C.E. Image was taken From The Use and Abuse of P52: Papyrological Pitfalls in the Dating of the Fourth Gospel, HThR 98 (2005), 23-48, esp. p. 41

Nongbri writes of P.Mich. 5336, "Several individual letters resemble those of P52, and the overall impression is similar. The vertical spacing of the lines is more compressed, but the spacing between letters is comparable, as is the rough bilinearity." I would note that having a dated manuscript of 152 C.E. only helps Roberts' date range of 100–150 C.E.

The problem with Nongbri's newfound manuscripts used for comparison is that they are all documentary texts being compared with the literary text of P52. Nongbri himself appears to admit their shortcomings when he writes, "Turner (Greek Manuscripts of the Ancient World, 19-20) notes that the ideal situation would be to compare literary hands to other dated literary hands. Unfortunately, examples of literary papyri with firm dates are in short supply, especially relative to the number of dated documentary papyri (see further the discussion in Roberts, Greek Literary Hands, xii-xv)." (Bold mine) All early Greek New Testament manuscripts, specifically the early papyri since that is our subject matter here, are literary documents, which means that they do not contain dates. Documentary texts, that is, manuscripts with documentary information, provide dates, often explicitly so. Or, at a minimum, they have something written within that document that can lead to a dating period. These documentary texts are therefore not as valuable as the literary documents when the comparison is with another literary document, which Nongbri seems to admit on the one hand and then complain about comparing literary with literary. I would also remind the reader that be it comparing literary text with documentary texts or literary with literary texts, this is paleographically dating the manuscripts. If we recall, Nongbri wrote, "Paleography is not the most effective method for dating texts, particularly those written in a literary hand.49 Roberts himself noted this point in his edition of P52." Yet, Nongbri, in this very paper, is using paleography to redate or length the date period of the P52.

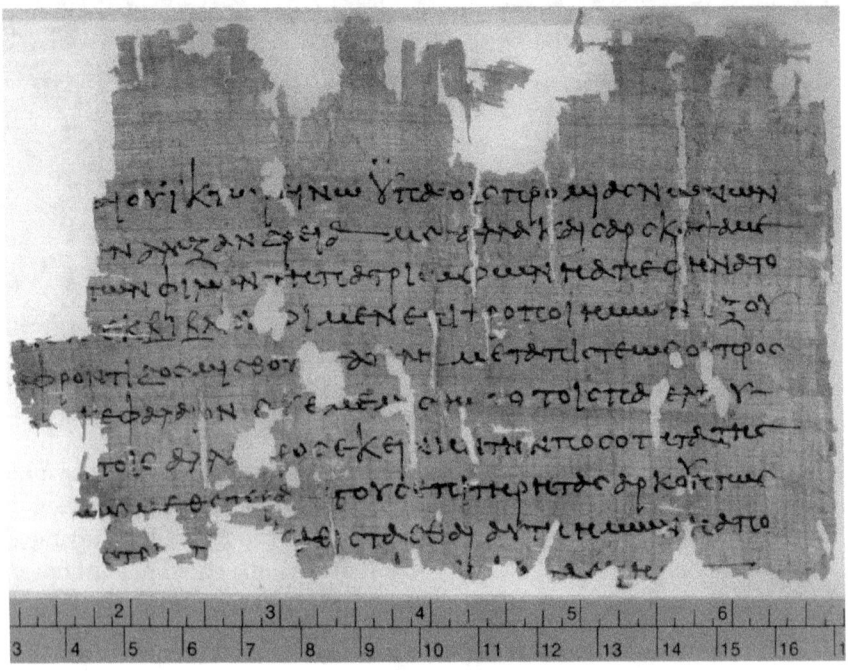

Image P.Oxy.LI 3614 Dating after 6 March (?) 200 Retrieved Wednesday, May 20, 2020 from http://www.papyrology.ox.ac.uk/POxy/

"A more cursive document that bears some resemblance to P52 is P.Oxy. 51.3614. P.Oxy. 51.3614 shows more ligatures than P52, but the vertical and horizontal spacing is similar. Several individual letters also show affinities."

Image P.Oxy. 52.3694 dating 12 March 218-25 or 278 C.E. Retrieved Wednesday, May 20, 2020 from http://www.papyrology.ox.ac.uk/POxy/

Nongbri writes, "The hand of P.Oxy. 52.3694 is obviously less well formed and less regular than that of P52, but it is to be expected that a document would be written more quickly and less deliberately than a literary text."

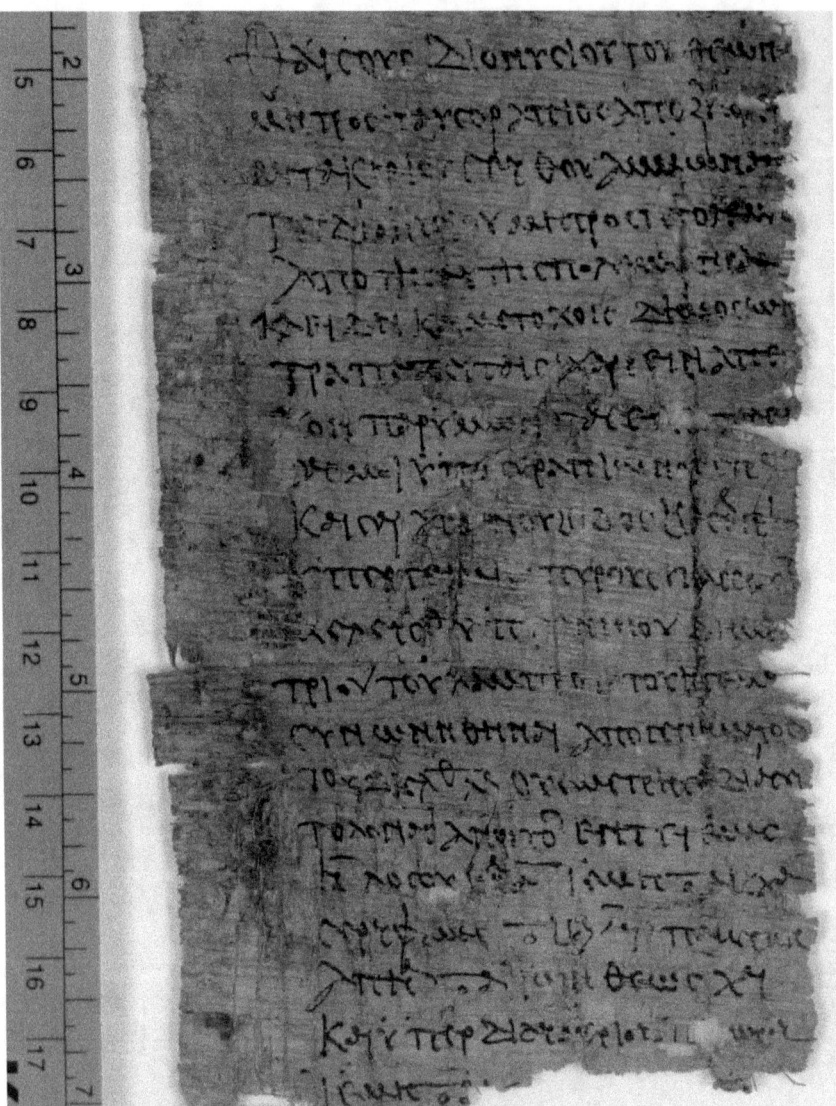

Image P.Oxy. 41.2968 dating between 28 August and 25 September A.D. 190. Retrieved Wednesday, May 20, 2020 from http://www.papyrology.ox.ac.uk/POxy/

What Nongbri said of P.Oxy. 52.3694, he said, also applies to P.Oxy. 41.2968, that is, both are "obviously less well-formed and less regular than that of P52, but it is to be expected that a document would be written more quickly and less deliberately than a literary text." Nongbri says that the upsilon is "very similar to those of P52, as is the mu." Agreed on the upsilon. He says that the rho is "also very close." I would disagree here.

THE P52 PROJECT

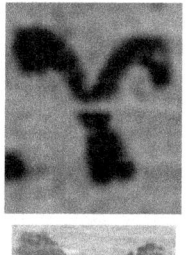
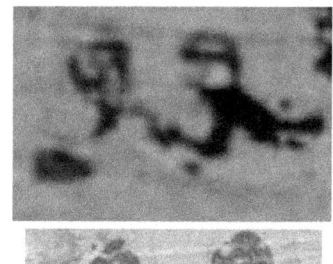
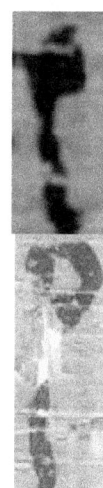

Image Upsilon-Mu-Rho from P.Oxy. 41.2968 and P52

While the upsilon here is similar, there is no ligature with P.Oxy. 41.2968 that we see with P52. Moreover, the upsilon P.Oxy. 41.2968. is also thicker. Yes, there are some similarities between the mu and rho, but there are also dissimilarities. While these letters have some similarities, overall, all the letterforms in P.Oxy. 41.2968 is quite different from P52. Moreover, the spacing between letters is different. The spacing between lines is different. Of P52, Nongbri writes, "The space between each line is about equal to the height of a line. There is an impression of a rough bilinearity." (bold mine) There is no effort on the part of the scribe of P.Oxy. 41.2968 to keep his text within an imagined upper and lower line, that is, a bilinear form.

What we are discovering with Nongbri's comparable manuscripts is those that have the closest comparable, that is, those that are most similar actually support a date of 94 to 150, which aligns with Roberts' range, and those manuscripts further removed to a later date range are far less similar to P52. Nongbri admits as much, "I have not radically revised Roberts's work. I have not provided any third-century documentary papyri that are absolute 'dead ringers' for the handwriting of P52."

Image P. Oxyrhynchus 2533 [early to middle second century]

The editors of P. Oxyrhynchus 2533 said that the handwriting was similar to first-century documents but that it has the appearance of a second-century document. Clearly the handwriting of this small portion of P. Oxyrhynchus 2533 is very much like P52.

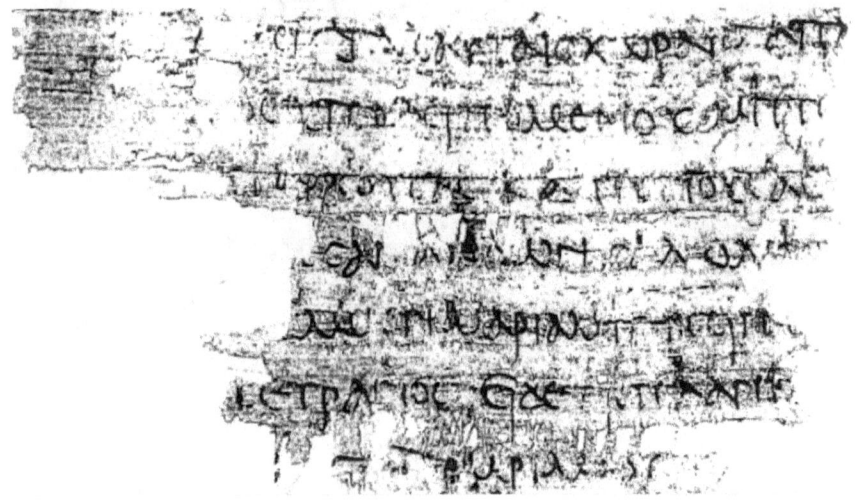

Image P. Murabba'at 113_Dated between 126-175 C.E.

The likeness between P52 and P. Murabba'at 113 is obvious, especially with the epsilon, iota, alpha, and the delta.

The paleographers and papyrologists of the last 20-30 years have a favorite saying, "follow the evidence," "you have to follow the evidence." Your response should always be "yes, follow the evidence, with one caveat, follow the weightiest evidence." You see dear reader they, the paleographers and papyrologists, are the arbiters of the evidence, so in some cases, it is simply manufactured weak evidence, or they are trying to overcome a mountain of old evidence with a new bucket of dirt.

Let us remember who is in the date range of 100-150 for P52: C. H. Roberts, Sir Frederic G. Kenyon, W. Schubart, Sir Harold I. Bell, Adolf Deissmann, E. G. Turner (cautiously), Ulrich Wilken, W. H. P. Hatch, Philip W. Comfort, and Bruce M. Metzger. Many manuscripts have been offered over the decades to support this long-held date range, and the greatest opponent, Brent Nongbri, openly admits, "I have not radically revised Roberts's work. I have not provided any third-century documentary papyri that are absolute 'dead ringers' for the handwriting of P52."

While I am not a reader of minds and hearts, we will leave that up to God Himself. Using my 32 years of work and some basic deduction, I would say Nongbri's article's title, and his beginning statement gives us his motivation for challenging such a long-standing date. The article title is "The Use and Abuse of P52." He then writes, "I can highlight the uncertainty involved in paleographic dating and encourage caution when using P52 to assess the date (and thus the social setting) of the Fourth Gospel." (pp. 26-27). He then concludes the article with, "The real problem is thus in the way scholars of the New Testament have used and abused papyrological evidence." (Nongbri, p. 46)

His entire motivation is derived from his belief that New Testament scholars have used and abused the dating range of 100–150 for P52. This is because for a long time before the discovery of P52, the Gospel of John was argued by liberal and moderate Bible scholars to have been written in about 170 C.E. This argument came to a screeching halt the moment P52 was dated between 100–150 C.E. The Gospel of John was now dated to the first half of the second century C.E., which is only a few decades after the original was written in about 98 C.E. In addition, it had made its way down in Fayum or Oxyrhynchus, Egypt. This meant that liberal to moderate Bible scholarship had no leg to stand on in their effort to dislodge John as the author of the Gospel. Many New Testament scholars would say that P52 was copied about 110 or about 125 C.E., a mere quarter of a century or so after John's death. Nongbri thinks two things: (1) it is abuse for the NT scholars to pick an arbitrary early part of the date range when discussing it and that (2) fifty years is too small of a date range.

So, he has set out to bring forward a handful of manuscripts to try and unseat that 100-150 C.E. date range of P52. He also brings forward an ad hominem attack on Roberts' age and experience. Yet, he knows that Roberts' upheld his initial dating decade after decade of his illustrious career until he died in 1990. His fear of what NT Bible scholars might do in using and abusing the 50-year date range is nothing in comparison to the textual scholars, paleographers, and papyrologists now falling in line and referring to the longer date range, and largely referring to the end of it, saying P52 should be dated to 200 C.E. earliest or later. You will notice that Nongbri and company are not offended at that use and abuse. Those new manuscripts actually point more to Roberts' dating of P52 than anything else. Nongbri is living in a world of probabilities based on scant evidence, which he openly admits as opposed to reality. His skeptic nature, pessimism, uncertainty, and ambiguousness result from postmodernism.

Their idea is that we can never be certain of anything regarding the Scriptures. Everyone knows that paleographic dating is conditional and difficult. No one has argued that paleographical dating is the "most effective method." Thus, it is a red herring fallacy to suggest that someone has argued that paleographical dating is the "most effective method" and then undermine what no one has actually claimed. It is a far cry from "not the most effective" to being ineffectual. Uncertainty does not displace levels of probability. When Nongbri suggests that "paleography is not the most effective method for dating texts," he seems to suggest that there is a better method readily available to us with P52, a literary undated document. Not only does Nongbri know this is not the case, but he also admits it himself, and then he turns to use paleography to undermine the 100–150 C.E. dating of P52. He well knows almost all New Testament manuscripts, which are literary undated documents, are dated strictly on paleographical bases.

Recently Brent Nongbri has argued that the dating of P75 to 175-225 C.E. is not reasonable. Instead, he argues that the similarity of the text of P75 to that of Codex Vaticanus is better explained in that, according to him, they were both produced in the fourth century C.E. P75 contains Luke 3:18–24:53 as well as John 1–15. Here we are with the Gospel of John again. Nongbri has also redated P66, a near-complete codex of the Gospel of John, from 150 C.E. to "early or middle fourth century" (300-350 C.E.). I am starting to see a pattern here when it comes to the Gospel of John. Nongbri's skepticism is unwarranted.

Color Plates of the Recto and Verso of P52

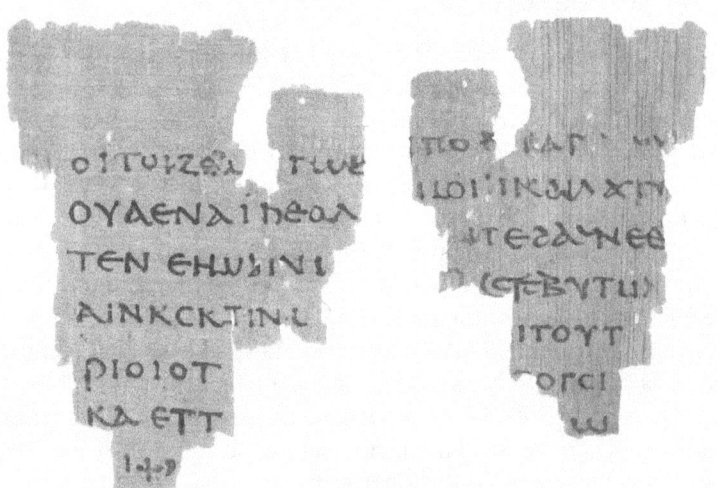

Appendix: Color Plates of the Recto and Verso of P52

THE P52 PROJECT
PHOTOGRAPHS OF THE EARLY MANUSCRIPTS

Image P. 6845 Homer, Ilias 8, 433-447 75-125 C.E. - Roberts

Image P52 Rylands Greek P 457 Recto

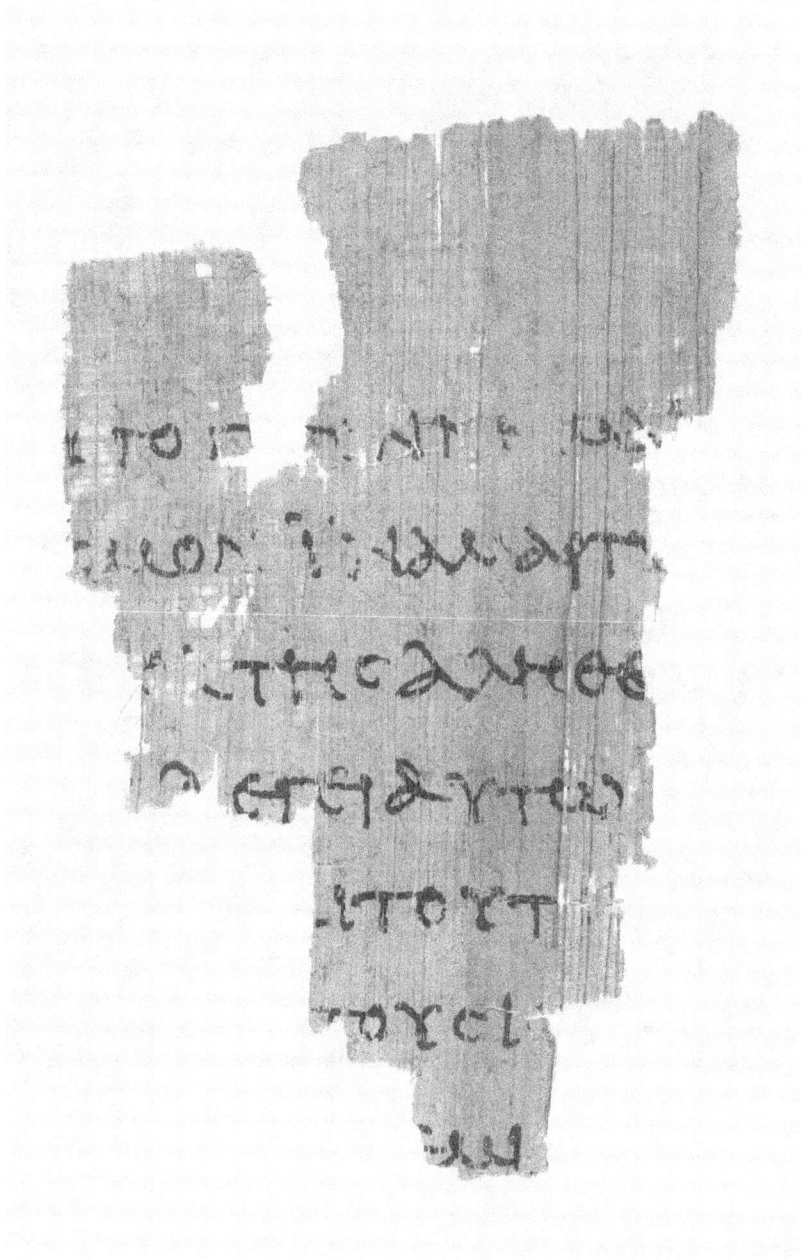

Image P52 Rylands Greek P 457 Verso

Image P. Egerton 2 The Unknown Gospel

THE P52 PROJECT

τον μεγεθος πολλακι
μεινει τουτον δε ως
λιτηγνυσιτιναστ
ηντεινταδεμε
ιτανεφι· διαβαρε
     δε
εσταπεζιωκαιτυ
αντερω πολιεσε
ονηπιψυχροτα
λαιτιτιτ του
εργαζομενον ο
ιππον τσεχ
υληνκαιαυτην
τηινυσαλιτωδ
ιερο σλεισιοπλη
ναυετιωτεροσασ
τωπρωμεγαστιν
ενιοιυ ητωνιναμ
ονηιηαρχομενοσ

Image Oxyrhynchus 3721 A HUTHOR: *Theophrastus, On Winds 4-7 ed. M. W. Haslam*

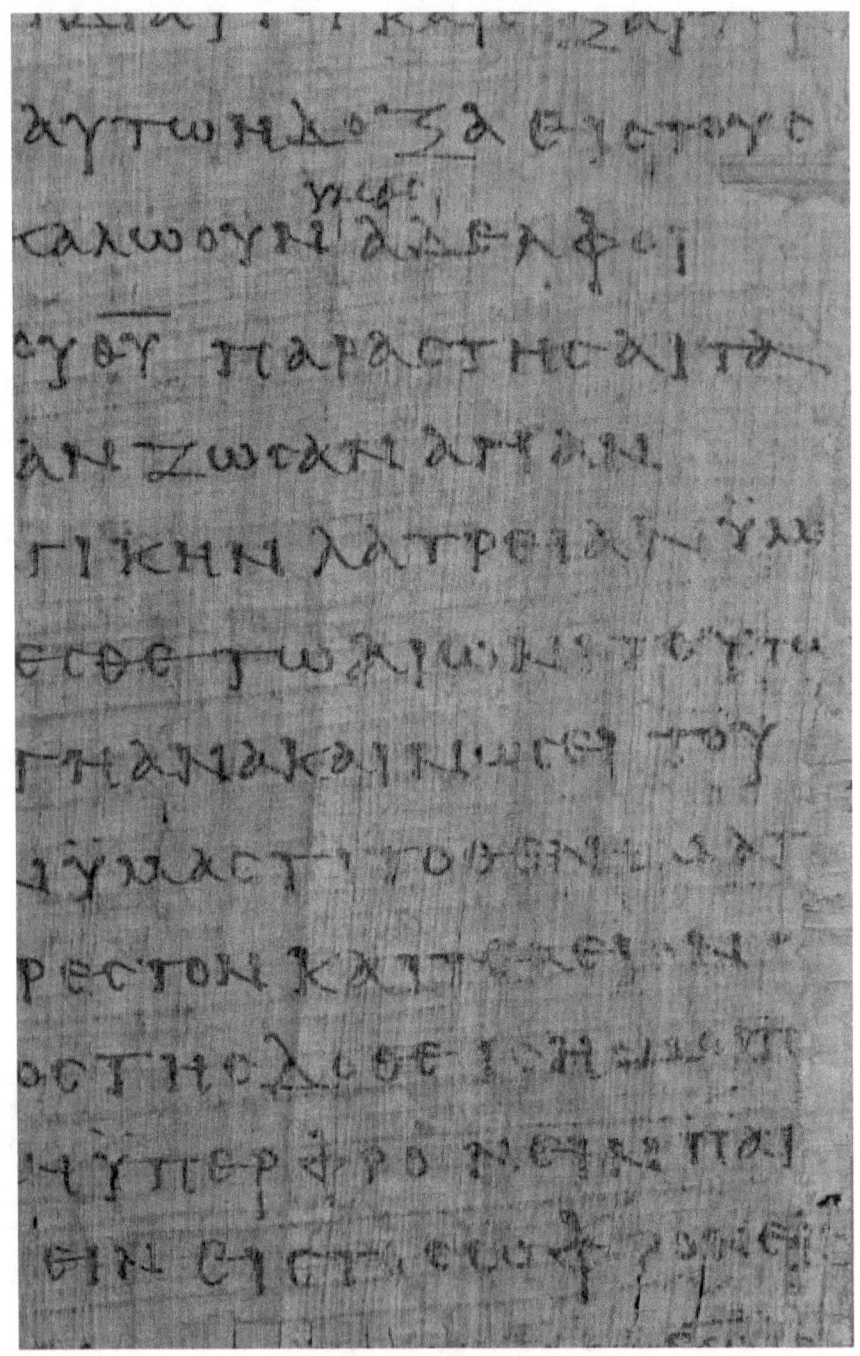

Image P46 containing most of the Pauline epistles

THE P52 PROJECT

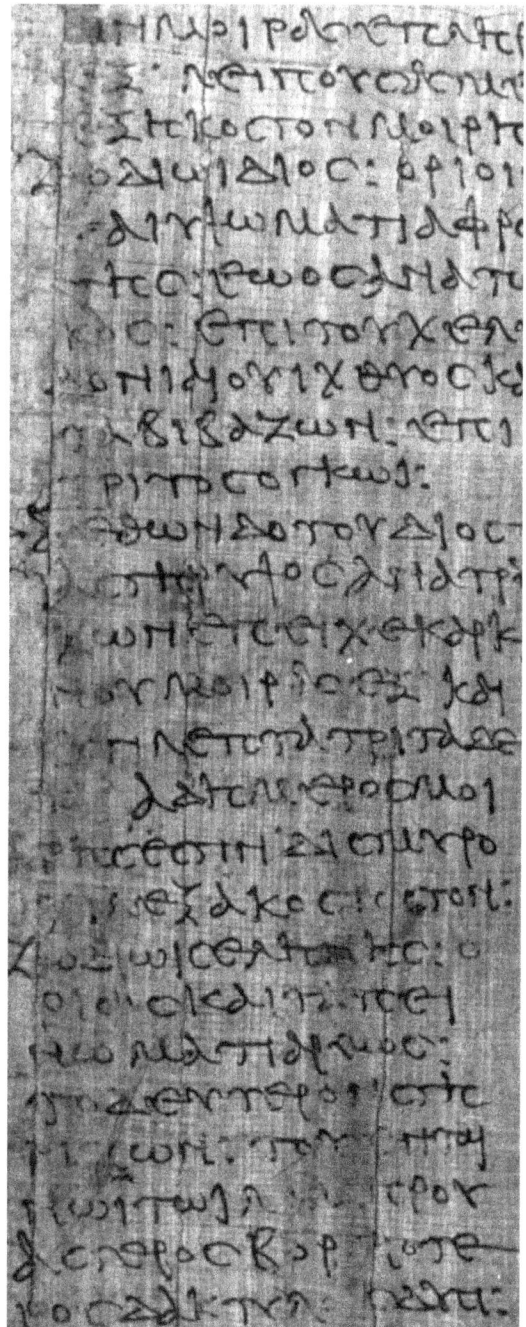

Image P. London 130 Horoscope, letter, teacher (astrology) to students

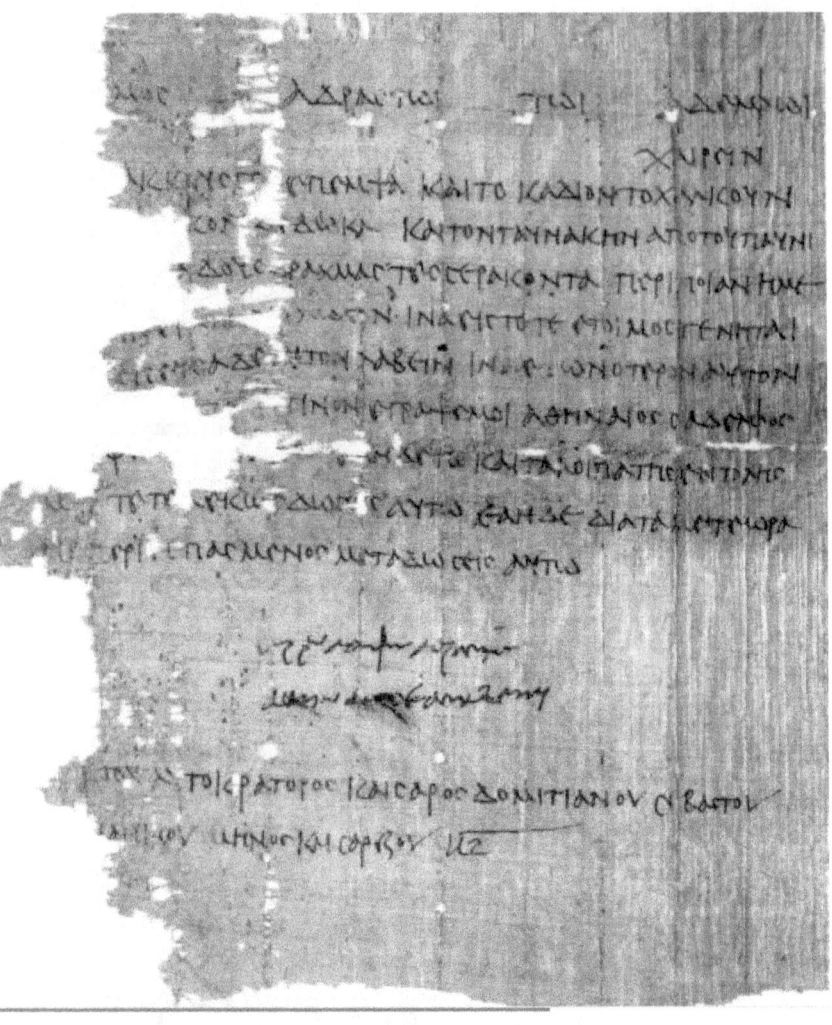

Image P. London 2078 a private letter written in the reign of Domitian (81-96 C.E.)

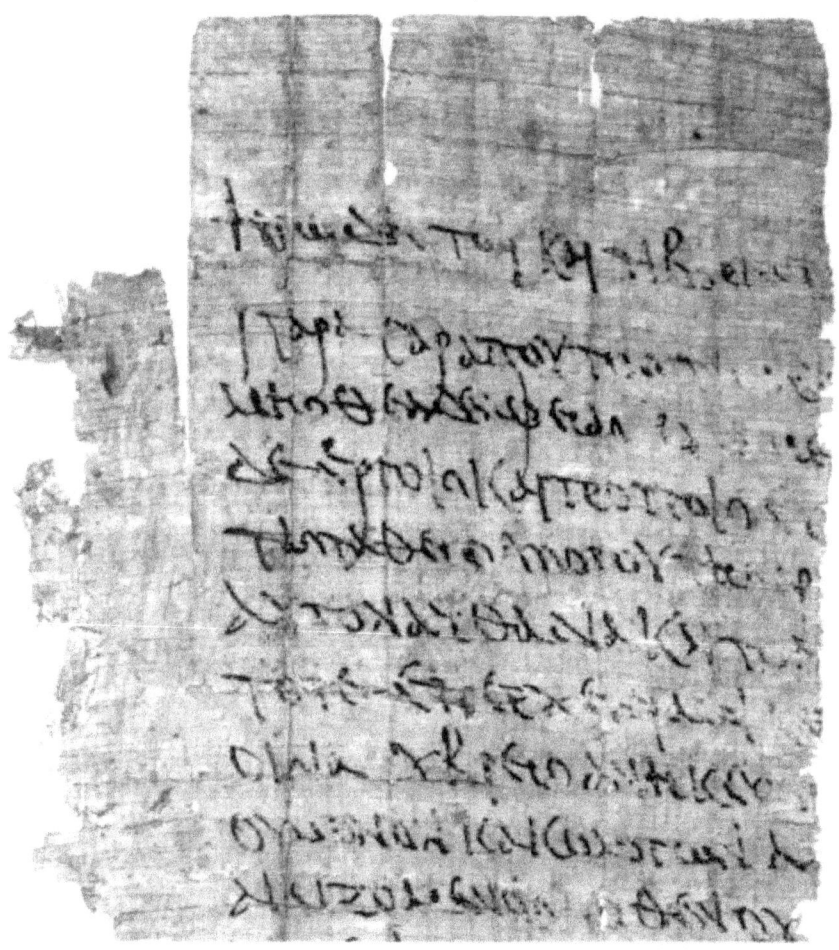

Image P. Oslo 22, a petition dated 127 C.E., House at Oslo University Library

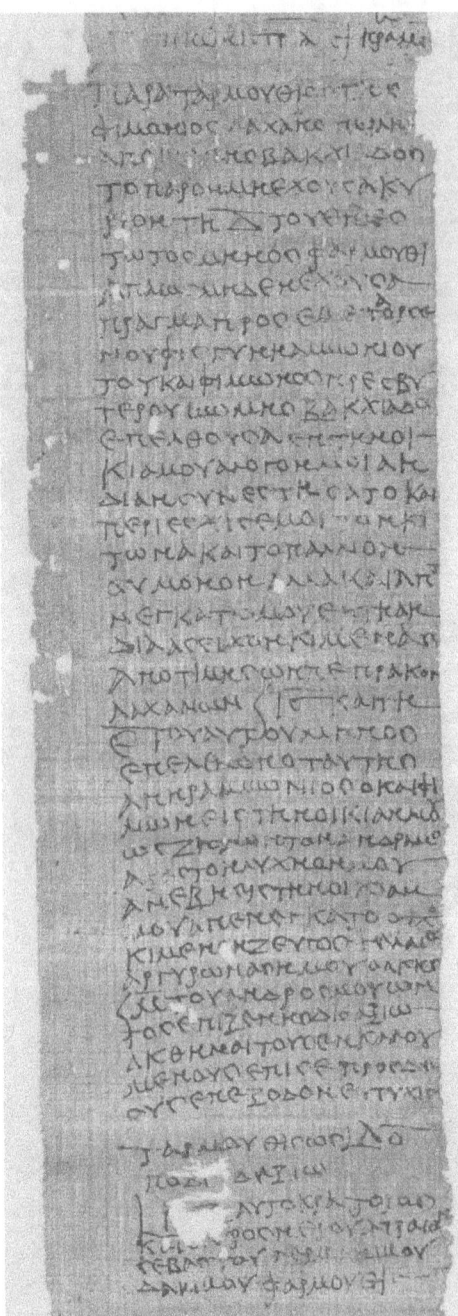

Image (B.G.U. 1.22) P_06854_R_001
dated to 114 C.E. Retrieved Tuesday, May 19, 2020
from http://berlpap.smb.museum/record/

THE P52 PROJECT

Image P.Mich.inv. 5336

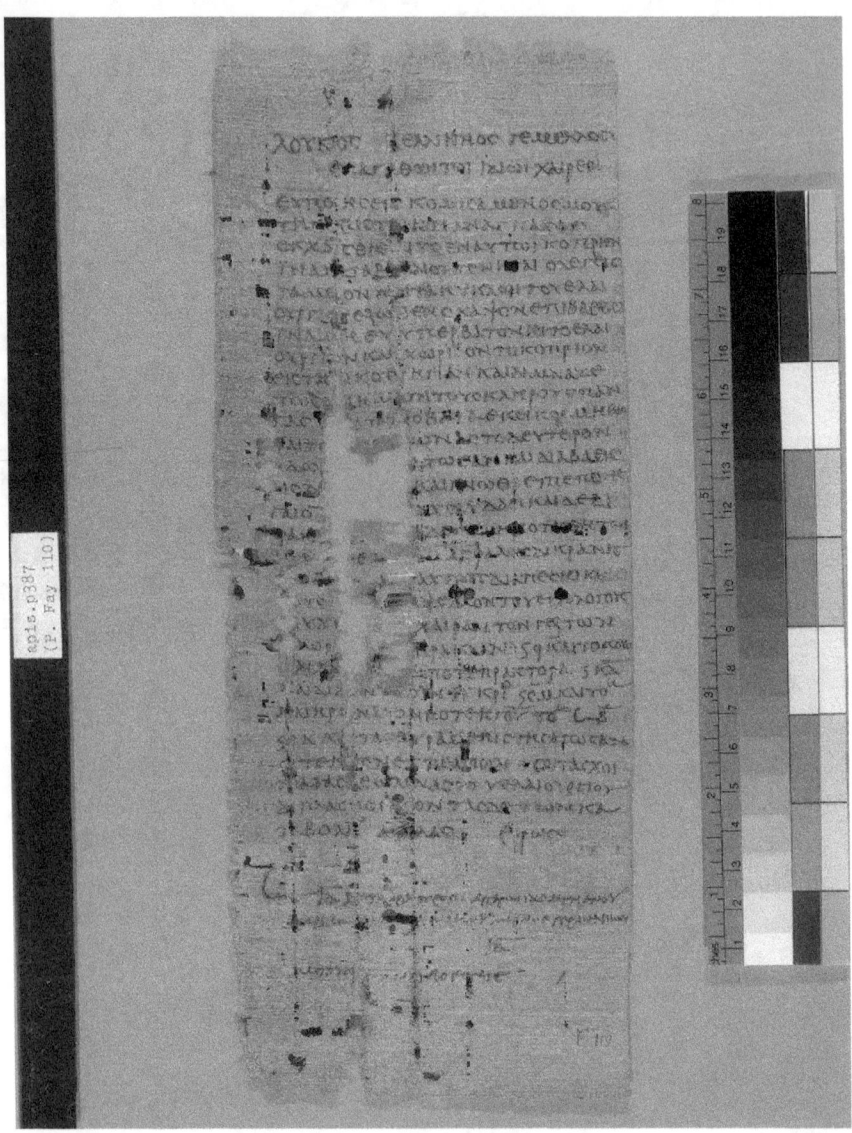

Image Pi P. Fayum 110 - 94 C.E. Dated (Letter from Gemellus to Epagathus)

THE P52 PROJECT

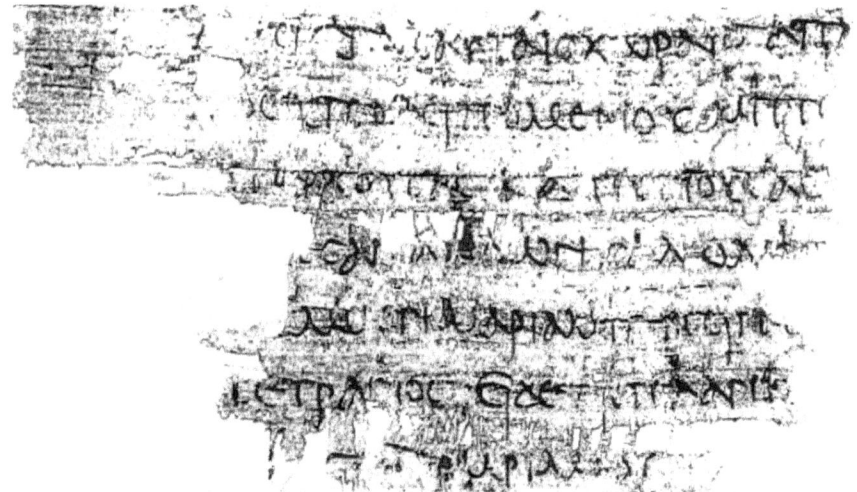

Image P.Mur. 2 113 (P. Murabba'at 113) Dated to 126 – 175 C.E.

Image P.Oxy.8 Papyrus Oxyrhynchus 8 (P. Oxy. 8) is a fragment of Greek hexameter poetry dated to the first or second century C.E.

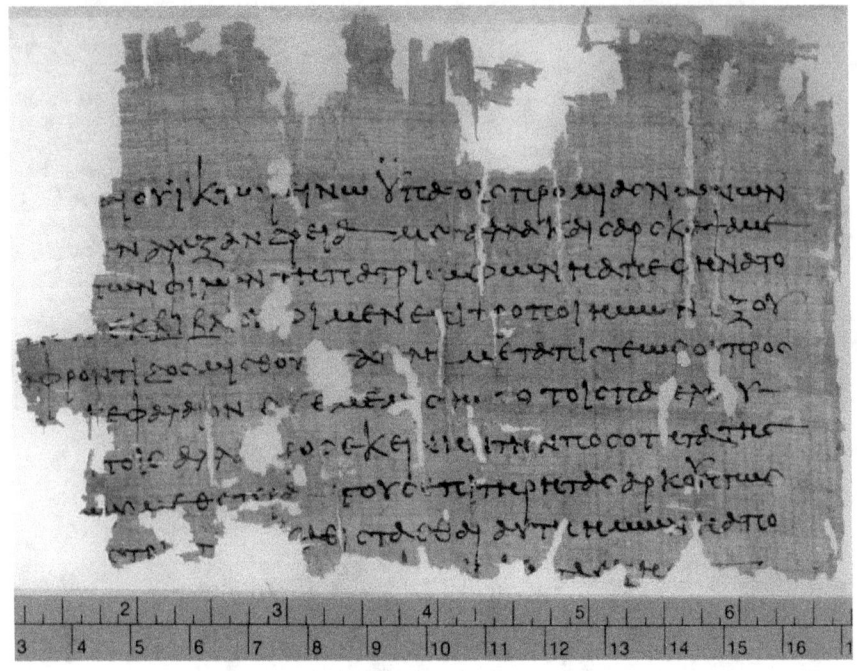

Image P.Oxy.LI 3614 dated to After 6 March (?) 200

THE P52 PROJECT

Image P.Oxy.XXXI 2533 dated to second century C.E. (Frame a.01)

Image P.Oxy.XXXI 2533 dated to second century C.E. (Frame b.01)

THE P52 PROJECT

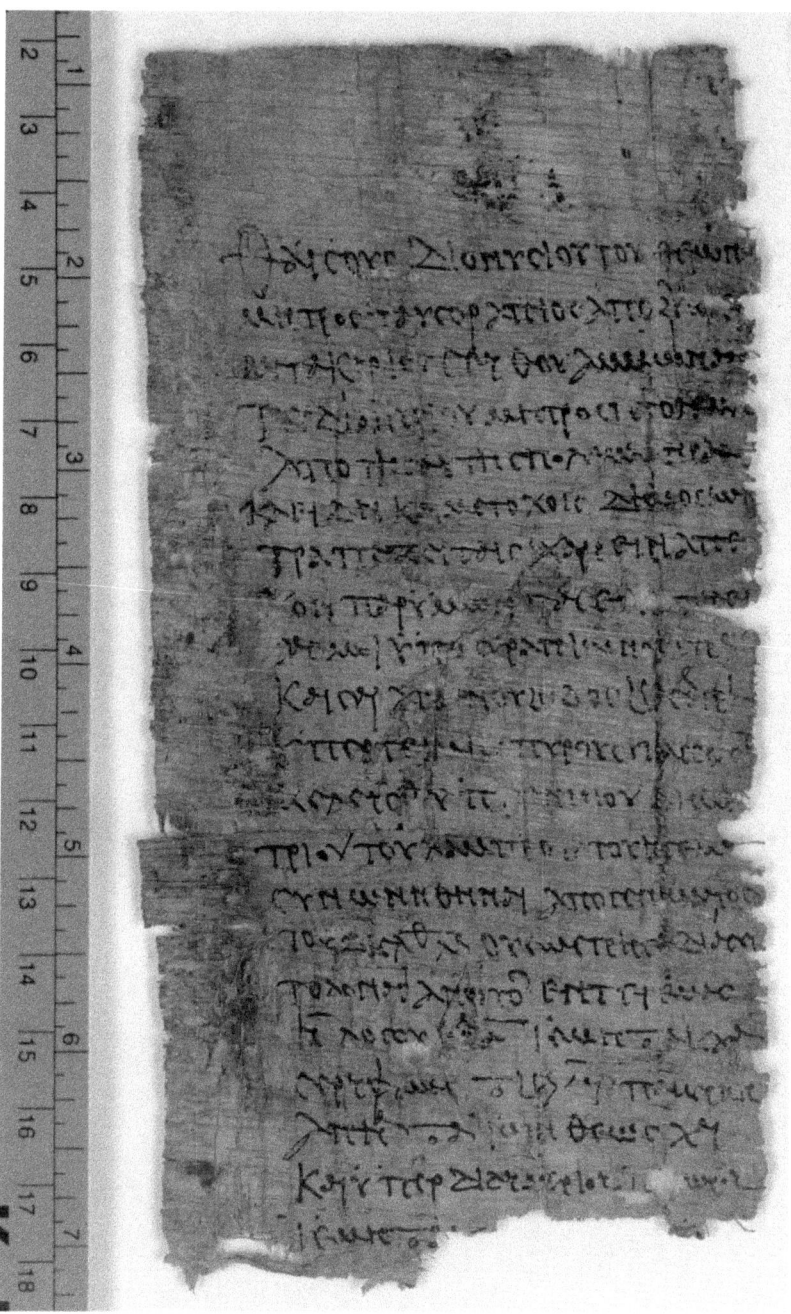

Image P.Oxy. 41.2968 dating between 28 August and 25 September A.D. 190

Image P.Oxy. 52.3694 dating 12 March 218-25 or 278 C.E.

THE P52 PROJECT

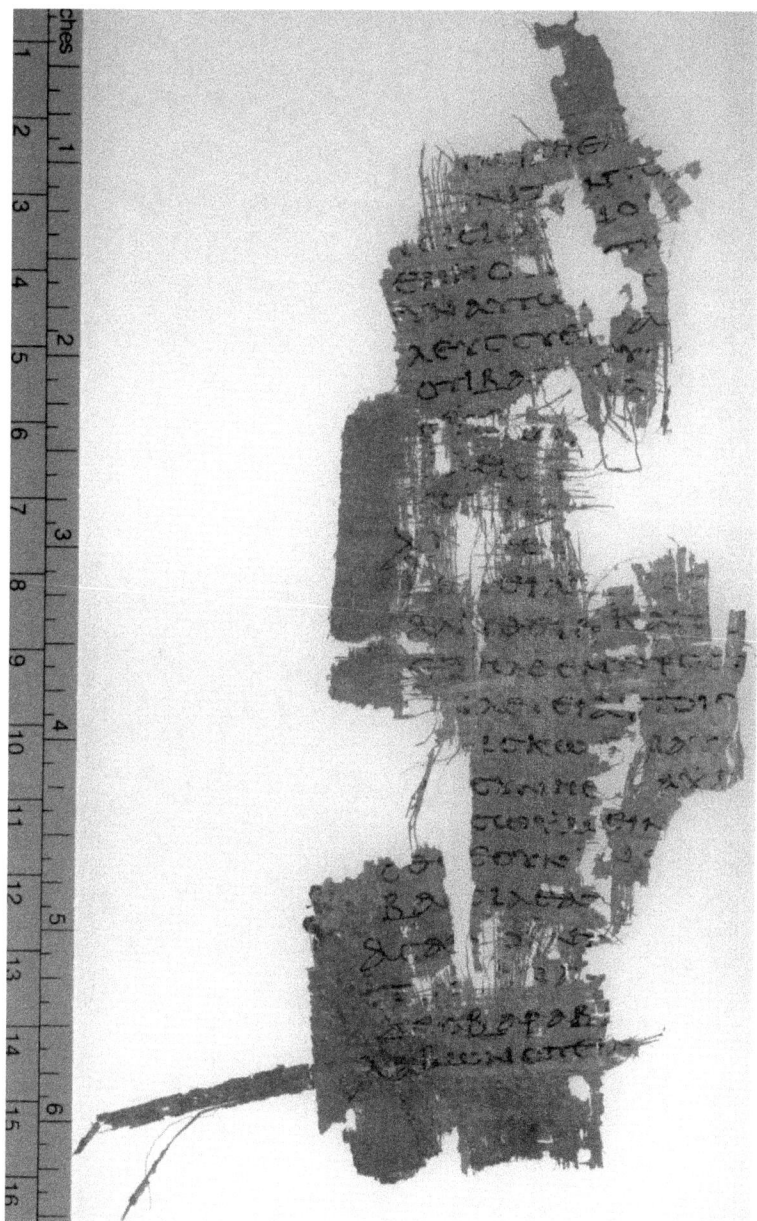

Image P.Oxy. L 3523 - Second Century - a

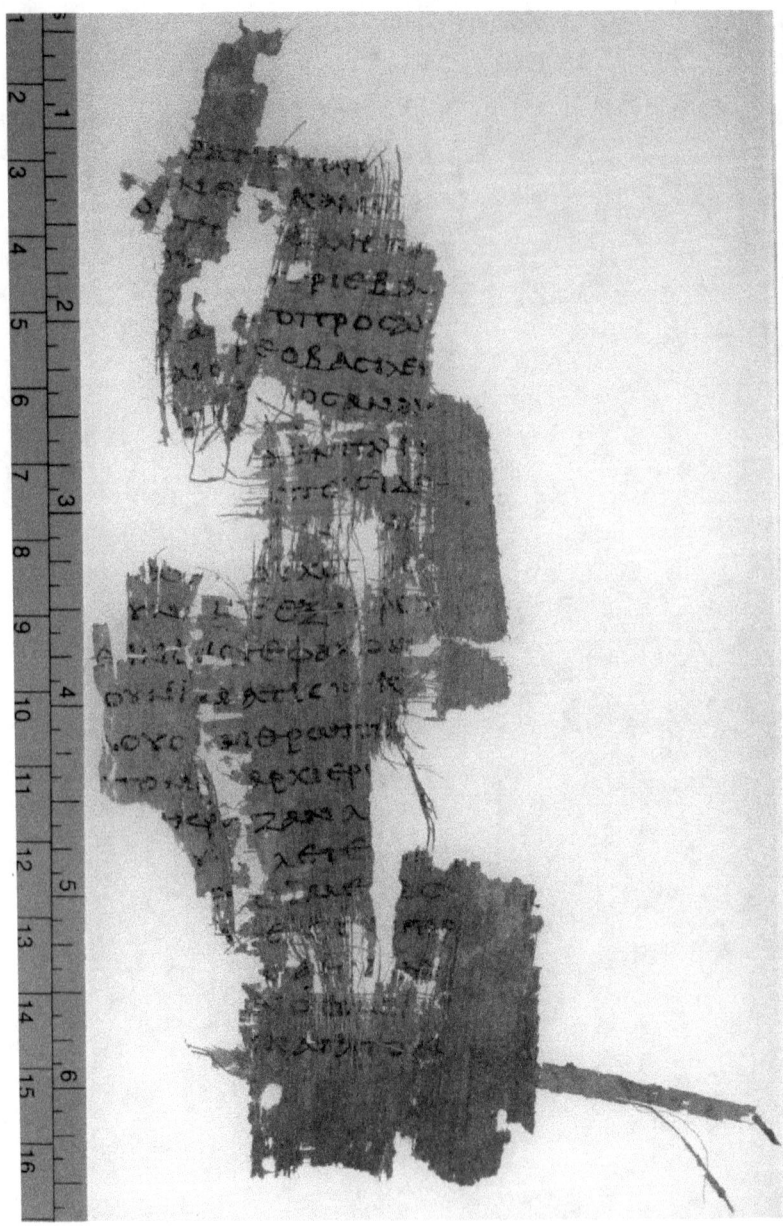

Image P.Oxy. L 3523 - Second Century - b

THE P52 PROJECT

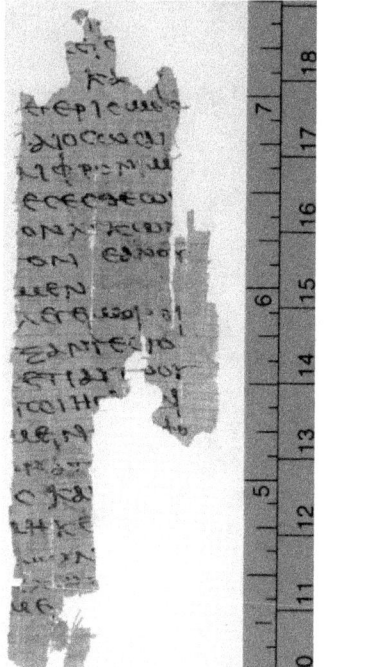

Image 1 P.Oxy. LX 4009 2nd cent. a

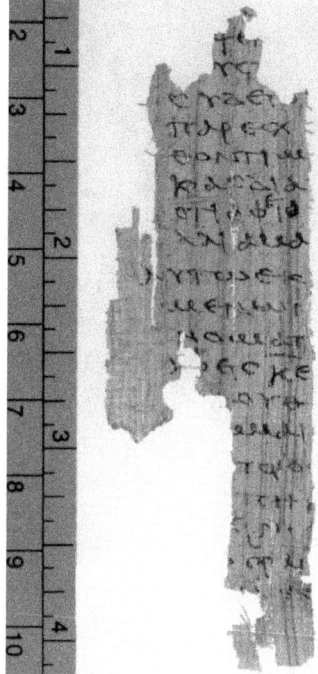

Image 2 P.Oxy. LX 4009 2nd cent. b

Image P.Oxy. LXIV 4404 late 2nd cent a

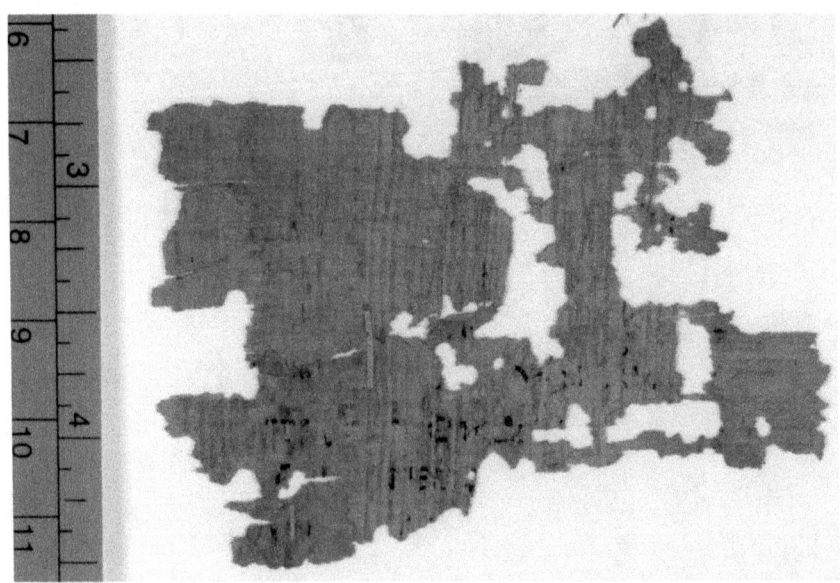

Image P.Oxy. LXIV 4404 late 2nd cent b

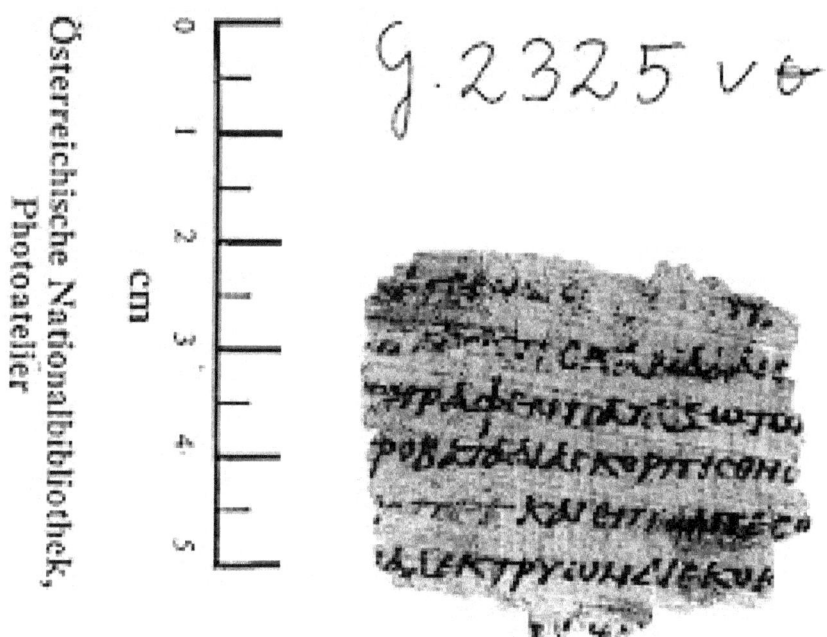

Image P.Vindob. G. 2325 estimated to date to 70-200 C.E. (commonly called the "Fayyum Fragment")

Image PSI V 446 date September 5 133/136 AD

THE P52 PROJECT
Highly Recommended Publication

The manuscripts that form the Greek New Testament are scattered throughout the world and are usually only accessible to scholars and professionals. These were the manuscripts read by the earliest Christians, which comprised their "New Testament." In his volumes, Philip Wesley Comfort bridges the gap between these extant copies and today's critical text by providing accurate transcriptions of the earliest New Testament manuscripts, with photographs on the facing pages so readers can see the works for themselves. Comfort also provides an introduction to each manuscript that summarizes the content, date, current location, provenance, and other essential information, including the latest findings. This allows students and scholars to make well-informed decisions about the translation and interpretation of the New Testament.

Volume 1 includes manuscripts from Papyrus 1-72. Volume 2 includes manuscripts from Papyrus 75-139 as well as from the uncials. In addition, it features a special section on determining the date of a manuscript. This two-volume set replaces the previously published single volume Text of the Earliest New Testament Greek Manuscripts, as it contains many new manuscripts, updated research, and higher quality images of all manuscripts previously covered.

Edward D. Andrews

Other Related Books By Edward D. Andrews

Bibliography

Bagnall, R. S. (2009). *Early Christian Books In Egypt*. Princeton, NJ: Princeton University Press.

Bagnall, R. S. (2009). *The Oxford Handbook of Papyrology*. New York, NY: Oxford University Press.

Barker, D. (2011). The Dating of New Testament Papyri. *New Testament Studies 57*, 571-82.

Cavallo, G. (2005). Il calamo e il papiro. La scittura greca dall'eta ellenistica ai primi secoli di Bisanzio, Florence. *Papyrologica Florentina 36*.

Comfort, P. W. (2005). *ENCOUNTERING THE MANUSCRIPTS: An Introduction to New Testament Paleography and Textual Criticism*. Nashville, TN: Broadman & Holman.

Comfort, P. W., & Barrett, D. P. (2019). *The Text of the Earliest New Testament Greek Manuscripts*. Grand Rapids, MI: Kregel Academic.

Hurtado, L. W. (2003). P52 (P.Rylands Gr 457) and the Nomina Sacra; Method and Probability. *Tyndale Bulletin*, 54.1.

Hurtado, L. W. (2019). *TEXTS AND ARTIFACTS: Selected Essays on Textual Criticism ans Early Christian Manuscripts*. New York, NY: T & T Clark.

Nongbri, B. (2008). The Use and Abuse of P52: Papyrological Pitfalls in the Dating of the Fourth Gospel. *Harvard Theological Review 98*, 1, 23-48.

Orsini, P., & Clarysse, W. (2012). Early New Testament Manuscripts and Their Dates: A Critique of Theological Palaeography. *Ephemerides Theologicae Lovanienses (ETL 88/4)*, 443–474.

Porter, S. E. (2013). Recent efforts to Reconstruct Early Christianity on the Basis of its Payrological Evidence. In *Christian Origins and Graeco-Roman Culture* (pp. 71–84). Leiden: Brill.

Porter, S. E. (2015). *John, His Gospel, and Jesus In Pursuit of the Johannine Voice*. Grand Rapids, MI: Wm. B. Eerdmans Publishing Co.

Roberts, C. H. (1935). *An Unpublished Fragment of the Fourth Gospel in the John Rylands Library*. Manchester, England: Manchester University Press.

Roberts, C. H. (1979). *Manuscript, Society and Belief in Early Christian Egypt.* Oxford, England: Oxford University Press.

Thompson, E. M. (1912). *An Introduction to Greek and Latin Paleaography.* Oxford: Clarendon Press.

Tuckett, C. M. (2001). P52 and Nomina Sacra. *New Testament Studies 47*, 544-48.

Turner, E. G. (1971). *Greek Manuscripts of Antiquity.* Oxford: Oxford University Press.

www.ingramcontent.com/pod-product-compliance
Lightning Source LLC
LaVergne TN
LVHW020930090426
835512LV00020B/3300